APPLIED MAINLINE ECONOMICS

ADVANCED STUDIES IN POLITICAL ECONOMY

Series Editors: Virgil Henry Storr and Stefanie Haeffele-Balch

The Advanced Studies in Political Economy series consists of republished as well as newly commissioned work that seeks to understand the underpinnings of a free society through the foundations of the Austrian, Virginia, and Bloomington schools of political economy. Through this series, the Mercatus Center at George Mason University aims to further the exploration and discussion of the dynamics of social change by making this research available to students and scholars.

Nona Martin Storr, Emily Chamlee-Wright, and Virgil Henry Storr, *How We Came Back: Voices from Post-Katrina New Orleans*

Don Lavoie, *Rivalry and Central Planning: The Socialist Calculation Debate Reconsidered*

Don Lavoie, *National Economic Planning: What Is Left?*

Peter J. Boettke, Stefanie Haeffele-Balch, and Virgil Henry Storr, eds., *Mainline Economics: Six Nobel Lectures in the Tradition of Adam Smith*

Matthew D. Mitchell and Peter J. Boettke, *Applied Mainline Economics: Bridging the Gap between Theory and Public Policy*

APPLIED MAINLINE ECONOMICS

Bridging the Gap between Theory and Public Policy

**MATTHEW D. MITCHELL
AND PETER J. BOETTKE**

 **MERCATUS CENTER**
George Mason University

Arlington, Virginia

ABOUT THE MERCATUS CENTER

The Mercatus Center at George Mason University is the world's premier university source for market-oriented ideas—bridging the gap between academic ideas and real-world problems.

A university-based research center, Mercatus advances knowledge about how markets work to improve people's lives by training graduate students, conducting research, and applying economics to offer solutions to society's most pressing problems.

Our mission is to generate knowledge and understanding of the institutions that affect the freedom to prosper and to find sustainable solutions that overcome the barriers preventing individuals from living free, prosperous, and peaceful lives.

Founded in 1980, the Mercatus Center is located on George Mason University's Arlington and Fairfax campuses.

Mercatus Center at George Mason University
3434 Washington Blvd., 4th Floor
Arlington, VA 22201
703-993-4930
mercatus.org

Cover and interior design by Joanna Andreasson, Brooklyn, NY
Typesetting and composition by Westchester Publishing Services, Danbury, CT
Index by Connie Binder, Laurel, MD

Library of Congress Cataloging-in-Publication Data

Names: Mitchell, Matthew D., author. | Boettke, Peter J., author.
Title: Applied mainline economics : bridging the gap between theory and public policy / Matthew D. Mitchell and Peter J. Boettke.
Description: Arlington, Va. : Mercatus Center at George Mason University, [2017]
Identifiers: LCCN 2016049099 (print) | LCCN 2016058187 (ebook) | ISBN 9781942951285 (pbk.) | ISBN 9781942951292 (Kindle ebook)
Subjects: LCSH: Economics. | Economic policy.
Classification: LCC HB171 .M549 2017 (print) | LCC HB171 (ebook) | DDC 330—dc23
LC record available at https://lccn.loc.gov/2016049099

CONTENTS

"In the study of society exclusive concentration on a speciality has a peculiarly baneful effect: it will not merely prevent us from being attractive company or good citizens but may impair our competence in our proper field. . . . The physicist who is only a physicist can still be a first-class physicist and a most valuable member of society. But nobody can be a great economist who is only an economist—and I am even tempted to add that the economist who is only an economist is likely to become a nuisance if not a positive danger."

—Friedrich A. Hayek, "The Dilemma of Specialization"

1
AN ENDURING PUZZLE

"No society can surely be flourishing and happy, of which the far greater part of the members are poor and miserable."

—*Adam Smith*[1]

HOW DO HUMAN societies work, and how can we make them work better? What methods, ideas, and strategies should we use to help us answer these questions? Economists have more empirical tools—more data and more sophisticated ways of testing those data—than ever before. We have randomized controlled trials and quasi-natural experiments; we have panel data methods and instrumental variables techniques. Adopted or adapted from the "hard sciences," these tools are designed to disentangle causation from correlation, and they promise to offer us a better understanding of human relationships. They are also popular with researchers and have become standard tools in the toolkit of the "mainstream" economist.

But unless those who employ these techniques also practice what we at the Mercatus Center at George Mason University call "mainline" economic thinking, these new empirical methods are liable to generate more heat than light. As the name implies, mainline economic thinking comprises the core tenets of economic knowledge. And though mainline concepts are constantly evolving, they draw their inspiration from, and are intimately connected with, the enduring lessons of early economic thinkers. A line connects the contemporary variants of these ideas to insights of Thomas Aquinas of the 13th century; the Scottish Enlightenment thinkers, such as Adam Smith, of the 18th century; and the Neoclassical School of the early 20th century. Thinkers in the last few decades have extended this line of inquiry, including Nobel laureates F. A. Hayek, James Buchanan, Ronald Coase, Douglass North, Vernon Smith, and Elinor Ostrom.[2] Mainline economics emphasizes that the market is a dynamic process, that institutional and cultural context shapes that process, and that political institutions are themselves the product of exchange. The mainline thinkers teach us that certain complex social orders compel self-interested men and women—as if by an invisible hand—to serve the interests of their fellows.[3] We use the term *mainline* in contrast with mainstream techniques that come and go, and it is our contention that these ideas ought to always be at the heart of economic analysis, irrespective of the latest trends.

In this book we summarize the ideas of mainline economics. Our goal is to introduce those working at the cutting edge of economic research and policy making to too-often-neglected concepts that offer a deeper understanding of the process of human interaction.

We begin with a puzzle that has vexed economists for more than 200 years, and we briefly survey the empirical tools that might answer this question. We show that this puzzle cannot be understood without grounding the analysis in theory, suggesting that the first place to start is with mainline economic theory.

We then discuss the core tenets of this theory. Throughout the discussion, we offer the reader examples of how these tools have helped researchers and policy analysts bridge the gap between ideas and real-world problems. Because these tools were synthesized and honed by researchers associated with George Mason University ("Mason"), we conclude with a brief history of that synthesis.

Why are some rich and others poor?

One question is perhaps the most important—and elusive—mystery in social science. It is the Big Question that Adam Smith set out to investigate more than 200 years ago: why are some societies fabulously wealthy while others are miserably poor?

The question calls out to us from the spreadsheets of international statistics that show that in 2015, the average Canadian produced 79 times as much (and therefore was able to consume roughly 79 times as much) as the average Burkinabe.[4] It is written in the historical record, which shows that—quite miraculously—the typical Western European's income grew 15-fold in just nine generations.[5] And the question is reflected in the actions of ordinary people, about 232 million of whom have left their home countries to seek their fortunes in more prosperous or peaceful lands.[6]

Prosperity matters. Greater wealth, of course, buys us nicer vacations and fancier gadgets. But it also buys us longer life spans.[7] It buys us better nutrition and lower infant mortality.[8] It buys more time with family and less time at work.[9] It buys greater self-reported happiness.[10] It makes us better stewards of the environment.[11] And it even buys intelligence, for as societies grow wealthier, their average IQs seem to rise.[12] As Harvard economist Benjamin Friedman has argued, wealth even seems to make us better people:

> Economic growth—meaning a rising standard of living for the clear majority of citizens—more often than not fosters greater opportunity, tolerance of diversity, social mobility, commitment to fairness, and dedication to democracy.[13]

Happily, greater income need not come at the expense of the least well off. World Bank economist Branko Milanovic calculates that the median earner in the United States earns more than 90 percent of the earth's inhabitants, and even the bottom 2 percent of US earners still earn more than 62 percent of the global population.[14] High and rising incomes do not solve all human problems. High-income societies have their share of maladies, including homelessness, obesity, and violence. But the overwhelming weight of evidence suggests that more economically prosperous societies have fewer and less severe problems.

Economists have offered many possible explanations

Prosperity matters. But how do we answer the Big Question? What *is* the source of economic prosperity? And what can those of us fortunate to live in prosperous societies do to help our less fortunate fellows? Economists have been trying to answer these questions since at least the time of Adam Smith. And every day, it seems, another clever economist suggests another answer.

Smith argued that prosperity was the result of specialization—which, he reasoned, depends on the extent of the market and on other factors, including institutions and geography. Economists in the past few decades have found support for Smith's observation.[15] Robert Solow developed a highly influential model that emphasized the importance of capital accumulation in growth.[16] Jeffrey Sachs and his coauthors have attributed prosperity to salubrious geographic and ecological factors such as climate, disease environment, and distance from the coast.[17] Jared Diamond, a professor of geography and physiology, proposed a similar thesis, focusing on the better natural endowments enjoyed by Europeans and Asians relative to American Indians, Africans, and Australians.[18] Gregory Clark has argued (quite controversially) that successful traits such as thrift and hard work have been passed down—or not—from generation to generation.[19] David Landes attributes differences in prosperity to differences in culture.[20] Daron Acemoglu and James Robinson, like Smith before them, attribute differences in outcomes to differences in institutions.[21] Joel Mokyr stresses access to technological ideas.[22] Deirdre McCloskey, like many others, credits individual liberty. "Liberated people, it turns out, are ingenious," she recently asserted in the *Wall Street Journal*.[23] But she also emphasizes cultural ideas. In particular, she asserts that when commerce is perceived as a dignified pursuit, societies thrive.[24]

How do we test these explanations?

How do we sort out the validity of these competing claims? Let's take a short tour through the standard empirical tools in the economist's toolkit, beginning with the least sophisticated and working our way up through more sophisticated, cutting-edge techniques.

Naïve correlations. The simplest way to assess these theories is to collect data and look for patterns. We might, for example, gather data on per capita GDP from the Penn World Tables and see how well the data correlate with certain institutional features, such as democracy, or certain interventions, such as foreign aid. The problem with this approach is that other factors (geography, culture, disease environment, history, etc.) might *also* affect per capita GDP, and simple correlations might accidentally pick up these confounding factors. For this reason, simple pairwise correlations are not actually very informative, even though they may be a good place to start.

Simple regression analysis. Economists have a handy tool that allows them to account for the influence of other factors. Known as "multivariable regression analysis," this technique theoretically allows us to measure, say, the effect of international aid on per capita GDP, *controlling for other factors, such as geography or institutions.*[25] Because human systems are so complex and other factors almost always matter, regression analysis has become an indispensable tool in quantitative economic analysis.

But simple regression analysis is not perfect. It requires a number of technical conditions to be true in order to yield unbiased estimates.[26] And when regression analysis fails to meet these technical conditions, it is often because researchers have failed to overcome what is known as the "identification problem." Simply put, this problem arises in complex systems when it is impossible to isolate cause and effect.[27]

The identification problem is an artifact of the special nature of economic data. Much like paleontologists or astronomers, economists typically work with observational data rather than with experimental data. With the latter, a researcher is able to run a randomized, controlled trial. In this case, a researcher can be reasonably certain that the identified effect (if any) is caused by the treatment applied to one set of observations and not to the control group.

But economists rarely have such a luxury. We cannot randomly assign half of the nations to be "treated" with well-protected property rights and the other half—a control group—to be subject to mediocre property protection. Instead, all we can do with simple regression analysis is observe those places that, by dint of historical luck, happen to have better protection of property rights and then compare outcomes in these places with outcomes in places with mediocre property protection. But if it turns out that property rights are not randomly determined and that those places with better protection of property rights are systematically disposed to have different cultures, different geographies, or some other unobserved difference, then a simple multivariable regression (even if it does attempt to control for other factors) may misidentify property rights as having a causal connection to prosperity. So empirical economists often turn to other techniques that allow them to solve the identification problem.

Experimental economics. In some cases, the identification problem can be avoided by eschewing observational data altogether. One night in 1956, economist Vernon Smith lay awake in a fit of insomnia. In the morning, he arose with an innovative idea: economics could be an experimental science.[28] He walked into his undergraduate class with a wad of cash and divided his students into buyers and sellers. He gave each buyer a card indicating his or her willingness to pay and each seller a card indicating his or her willingness to accept. The numbers written on the cards corresponded to actual cash that the students stood to gain through exchange (in other words, he invented supply and demand curves). Then he let the students trade on their own terms. To Smith's great surprise, the price that emerged in this market was the price predicted by the simple supply and demand model to maximize producer and consumer surplus.[29] Smith's experiment proved two things: first, in normal markets of perishable goods, market exchange tends to maximize welfare (even with relatively few buyers and sellers), and second, some economic questions can be tested in a laboratory setting. A half century later, Smith was awarded the Nobel Prize in Economics for these insights.

Since Smith's groundbreaking paper, experimental economists have conducted thousands of experiments, some yielding happy results (humans cooperate in social dilemmas far more than game theory would predict)[30] and others yielding unhappy results (bubbles invariably emerge in asset markets).[31] But not all questions lend themselves to laboratory experimentation. And unfortunately some of the most important questions—such as the Big Question—simply cannot be answered in the lab. In these cases, we are back to observational data.

Quasi-natural experiments. The problems with quantitative analysis of observational data have been well understood for decades.[32] But aided by better data and newer ways to test it, econometricians have recently responded to these critiques with earnest efforts to develop "identification strategies."[33] Simply put, the idea of an identification strategy is to *think like an experimenter* and to exploit random events or quasi-natural experiments to draw causal inference. Three techniques, in particular, have become popular in quasi-experimental designs: instrumental variables, regression discontinuity designs, and difference-in-differences analyses. Each of these techniques is best understood by way of example.

Instrumental variables. Steven Levitt wanted to know how additional police officers affect crime. But looking at simple correlations between officers per capita and crime per capita is not helpful because there is an omitted variable bias: places that are inherently violent for some (unobserved) reason will tend to have more crime *and* more officers to deal with that crime. Thus, the simple correlation suggests that more cops cause more crime! In an instrumental variables test, the researcher looks for some variable or variables—an instrument or instruments—that might cause variation in the variable of interest but is not directly related to the outcome variable. Levitt used mayoral election cycles as his instrument, exploiting the fact that politicians tend to put more police on the street before an election. This instrumental variables technique allowed him to obtain an unbiased estimate of the effect of police on crime. From this, he estimated that each additional officer eliminated between eight and ten crimes.[34]

Regression discontinuity designs. Economists Joshua Angrist and Victor Lavy wanted to study the effect of class size on student achievement. The problem is that class size is not randomly determined. Principals, acting on the belief that smaller classes are better, may assign low-performing students to smaller classes in the hopes of improving their performance. Thus, a simple correlation between class size and achievement might be tainted by reverse causality. In a regression discontinuity design, researchers exploit the fact that sometimes groups of people are treated differently on the basis of essentially arbitrary numerical cutoffs. In the 12th century, the rabbinic scholar Maimonides proposed a maximum class size of 40, and since 1969 Israeli public schools have followed this rule. This means that schools with just under a multiple of 40 enrollees (39, 79, 119, etc.) in a particular grade will tend to have just under 40 students per class, while schools with just over a multiple of 40 enrollees (41, 81, 121, etc.) in a grade will tend to have about 20 students per class. Since other differences between a school with 119 students in a grade and a school with 121 students in a grade are presumably random, Angrist and Lavy were able to exploit Maimonides's rule to estimate the effect of class size on student performance. Their regression discontinuity design allowed them to estimate that among fourth and fifth graders, smaller class sizes substantially increase test scores.[35]

Difference-in-differences analysis. Does the death penalty save lives by deterring murder? In 1972, the US Supreme Court found the death penalty to be unconstitutional, leading to its suspension. Four years later, the court reinstated the penalty. It would be tempting to look at this temporary moratorium as a natural experiment and to compare murder rates during this period to murder rates before and after. But there were so many other economic and cultural changes over this period that it would be difficult to attribute changes in the murder rate to the death penalty alone. In a difference-in-differences design, researchers compare changes over time in locations with a certain treatment to changes over time in other locations. John Donohue and Justin Wolfers employed this technique to examine the effect of the death penalty on murder. They examined the evolution of murder in the United States and Canada over this four-year period in which the United States suspended its death penalty while Canada's policy remained unchanged. (In Canada, the penalty only applies to the murder of on-duty law enforcement personnel and therefore is almost never used.) Donohue and Wolfers noted that while the US murder rate was consistently higher than that of Canada, the two rates moved in parallel fashion. Since the US murder rate seemed to evolve in much the same way as the Canadian murder rate over the period of the US death penalty moratorium, the authors concluded from this difference-in-differences design that capital punishment does little to deter murder.[36] When using a dataset with observations from multiple locations over multiple years (a time-series cross-sectional dataset) difference-in-differences estimates can be obtained by including sets of dummy variables for regions and years.[37] Since these sorts of datasets are becoming more prevalent, this technique has quickly become the most-used identification strategy.

But measurement without theory is impossible

These techniques are not new; the earliest known attempt to solve the identification problem dates back to economist Philip Wright's early use of instrumental variables in 1928.[38] But the techniques are now quite popular, and their popularity has led econometricians Joshua Angrist and Jörn-Steffen Pischke to claim that we are witnessing a "credibility revolution in empirical economics."[39] It is tempting to think that this revolution permits us to practice what the Nobel laureate economist Tjalling Koopmans once critically called "measurement without theory."[40] As another Nobelist, economist James Heckman, recently put it, "It's very appealing to say, 'let's not let the theory get in the way. We have all the facts. We should look at facts.'"[41] But as Koopmans, Heckman, and many others have averred, measurement without theory is impossible and to think otherwise is unwise. In this section, we offer a number of reasons for why theory is necessary if we are to understand measured facts.

First, measurement without theory is impossible because data require interpretation. Milton Friedman, a consummate empiricist, offers a nice example.[42] Imagine you have a house located in a climate with highly volatile temperature. Imagine, further, that you have a thermostat that alternatively turns on the heat and AC to ensure that the rooms of the house remain at 72 degrees Fahrenheit. If you looked at the naïve correlations, you'd incorrectly conclude that neither the outside temperature, the heater, nor the AC had any effect on the inside temperature. If you attempted a simple multivariate regression analysis, you again would not understand the true relationship because all of the explanatory variables would be perfectly collinear, a violation of ordinary least squares (OLS) assumptions.[43] To really understand what is going on, you must have some theoretical appreciation for the way a thermostat and ambient temperature work.

Second, to an even greater degree than simpler methods, the newly popular empirical techniques *require* theoretical understanding if they are to be used responsibly. As we've noted, many of these techniques are quite old. Economist Isaac Ehrlich's (often criticized) 1970s research on capital punishment employed instrumental variables. But, as Angrist and Pischke point out, Ehrlich "did not explain why these are good instruments, or even how and why these variables are correlated with the right-hand-side endogenous variables."[44]

Thus, Angrist and Pischke argue that the credibility revolution is not driven so much by the techniques themselves as by "the fact that research design has moved front and center in much of empirical micro."[45] In other words, most of the techniques (think of Levitt's study of police and crime) only yield unbiased estimates when the researcher has a deep understanding of the theoretical relationships between the variables.

Third, theory is necessary to appreciate how even the most careful randomization designs might be contaminated. One of the central theoretical insights of economics, in fact, invites contamination. This is the insight that humans respond to incentives. If a certain "treatment"—smaller class size, a job-training program, a breakthrough medicine—is hypothesized to have positive effects on human well-being, those who are assigned to the control group have a strong incentive to cheat the test and assign themselves back into the treatment group, undermining the researcher's careful attempt to randomize treatment.[46]

Fourth, and relatedly, human interaction is a dynamic and iterative process. Humans learn over time, and their reactions often change as they learn. This means that the underlying structural "parameters" of human behavior may not be stable, violating a key assumption of OLS estimation.[47] The Nobel laureate economist Robert Lucas famously pointed this out, noting that changing parameters make it especially difficult to draw policy conclusions from econometric estimations:

> Given that the structure of an econometric model consists of optimal decision rules of economic agents, and that optimal decision rules vary systematically with changes in the structure of series relevant to the decision maker, it follows that any change in policy will systematically alter the structure of econometric models.[48]

This "Lucas critique" requires that researchers be attuned to the institutional and cultural environment in which their studies take place. They must appreciate that whatever conclusions they draw may not be generalized to other settings, a problem that quantitative and experimental researchers refer to as the "external validity" problem.[49]

Fifth, and finally, given that there are a bewildering array of factors that might affect human behavior and maddeningly complex ways that these factors might interact, it is extremely difficult to reduce some important questions to a set of simple equations.[50] Trade, for example, may directly affect growth by permitting mutually beneficial exchange. But it might also indirectly affect growth by causing nations to be open to other types of policy change.[51] Geography may directly affect growth if it makes some places less susceptible to disease or more suitable to agricultural cultivation.[52] But, as Adam Smith emphasized, geographical configurations such as navigable rivers and miles of coastline might indirectly affect growth by permitting trade.[53] Or, to make matters even more complicated, geographical features such as oil deposits may affect the adoption of institutions that may affect policy choices that may then affect growth.[54]

The prevalence of so many nested relationships has caused development economists to emphasize that there are both "proximate" as well as "deep" sources of growth.[55] But disentangling the two can be very difficult. For example, Harvard economist Edward Glaeser and his colleagues argue that some researchers mistakenly give credit for policy outcomes to institutions—such as constitutional rules that constrain a leader's *ability* to expropriate property—when in fact some policy outcomes are the result of a dictator's *choice* to respect property rights.[56]

As we noted in the last section, researchers have attempted to disentangle these relationships with sophisticated "identification strategies." But sometimes regression analysis is unhelpful because there simply is no plausible identification strategy. The latest generation of empiricists exploits the fact that there are occasionally instances in which accidents of history cause some factor to vary randomly, making it easier to isolate and identify. But it is a frustrating fact of life that these quirks of history seem to be more common in trivial settings—where sumo wrestlers might cheat and game show contestants might be biased—than in more weighty matters.[57] It is nearly impossible to find a random quirk of history that causes one (and only one) institutional variable to be different in one place than in another, making it difficult to identify causal relationships. As Stanford economist Raj Chetty puts it, this means that far too many economists "think about the question less than the method."[58] But questions, Big Questions, are made no less big by the fact that they cannot be answered with an instrumental variable.

So economists must theorize

The Big Question remains unanswered over 200 years since Adam Smith first asked it. Despite the advent of the credibility revolution in econometric research, measurement without theory cannot offer credible answers to the question. And so, for the reasons we adumbrate above, the cutting edge of economic inquiry—which can and should avail itself of the latest quantitative techniques—must be guided by good theory.

In the remainder of this essay, we aim to acquaint the reader with what we believe are the best theories in economics. Though they continue to be refined and extended, these ideas are derived from mainline theories that have been at the core of economic thinking for centuries.

Our colleagues at the Mercatus Center and at the Economics Department at George Mason University regularly employ these theories to make sense of the world. Therefore, we include examples throughout our discussion of how their work helps bridge the gap between theory and real-world problems.

APPLICATION 1:
THE HIDDEN WEALTH OF NATIONS

About 140,000 Mexicans immigrate to the United States every year.[59] Many of them move just a few miles—enough to get themselves over the border—and those who make this move can expect to more than quadruple their earnings.[60]

Why is it that crossing an arbitrary line in the desert can yield a fourfold increase in pay?[61] The explanation begins with productivity. On an annual basis, a US worker produces about six times as much value as a Mexican worker.[62] And firms are willing to pay more productive workers more than less productive workers. But this explanation only reveals another mystery: why are workers in the United States so much more productive than workers in Mexico?

By focusing on those migrants who make the short leap across the US–Mexico border, we can eliminate a number of possible explanations. One's age, education, job history, skill set, work ethic, and marital status do not change when one crosses the border. Nor is there a large difference in the climate or natural resources just north of the border compared to just south of it.

Once they move, immigrants have access to more capital—faster computers and better machines—than they had in Mexico. And this accounts for something. But it turns out that cross-country differences in physical capital can only explain a fraction of the differences in cross-country earnings.[63]

As such, much of the wealth of nations cannot be seen, touched, or measured.[64] But theory—especially mainline theory—gives us some hints about what this intangible wealth might be. This theory tells us that when a Mexican crosses the border into the United States, he gains access not only to different machinery and tools but also to a different court system, a different system of taxation and regulation, and a different culture with alternative attitudes and customs toward exchange. In *Bourgeois Dignity*, a masterful account of the rise of modern growth, economic historian Deirdre McCloskey shines a light on some of these invisible sources of prosperity, especially the cultural attitudes toward exchange.[65] And in *Understanding the Culture of Markets*, Mercatus scholar Virgil Storr unravels the mystery of culture, helping us understand what it is and how it shapes our economic life.[66]

The annual migration across the Sonoran and Chihuahuan Deserts suggests that unseen differences matter. And mainline theory helps us understand what these differences might be.

2
THE CORE
THEMES OF
MAINLINE
ECONOMICS

"This division of labour, from which so many advantages are derived, is not originally the effect of any human wisdom, which foresees and intends that general opulence to which it gives occasion. It is the necessary, though very slow and gradual, consequence of a certain propensity in human nature which has in view no such extensive utility; the propensity to truck, barter, and exchange one thing for another."

—*Adam Smith*, The Wealth of Nations[1]

IN THE FOLLOWING pages, we organize our discussion of mainline economic thinking around three principal ideas: the market is a process, institutional and cultural context shapes that process, and these political institutions are themselves the product of exchange. The reader will note that each of these concepts roughly corresponds to a "school" of thought. These are, respectively, the Austrian school, the new institutional economics school, and the public choice school. As we emphasize in the final section, there are gains from intellectual exchange. And we believe it is more fruitful to focus on the blending of ideas than on the distinct "camps" that formulated them. We offer a starting place and a primer on each concept, while more exhaustive expositions can be found in the notes. We begin with six elements that clearly belong in all three schools of thought.

Exchange is mediated by human institutions

What is economics? Given that mainstream economists study everything from male-to-female population ratios[2] to the premium that Mexican clients are willing to pay prostitutes for unprotected sex,[3] it is tempting to agree with the late University of Chicago economist Jacob Viner, who is said to have defined economics as whatever it is that economists do.[4] It is useful, however, to draw a distinction between what is currently fashionable in mainstream economics and the core propositions of the discipline—what we call mainline economics.

The roots of mainline economics stretch deep into the past.[5] But today it is the hallmark of relatively recent Nobel-winning economists such as F. A. Hayek, James Buchanan, Ronald Coase, Douglass North, Vernon Smith, and Elinor Ostrom.[6] As we explain in section VII, these Nobelists were answering a challenge, issued by Hayek in 1949, to "make the building of a free society once more an intellectual adventure, a deed of courage."[7] Mainline economics can be summarized by three propositions:

1. As Adam Smith taught us, the market is a process, and it is driven by the human "propensity to truck, barter, and exchange one thing for another."[8]
2. The nature of this human exchange is profoundly influenced by the cultural norms and institutional rules within which it takes place.
3. Given the right institutional environment, the natural human tendency to exchange will lead to socially beneficial outcomes. But exchange itself shapes the institutional environment, and there is no guarantee that the right institutional environment will evolve.

Though the mainline approach emphasizes that market exchange often improves life, it differs from the unattainable ideal of "perfect competition" that one finds in many economics textbooks. Mainline economics does not, for example, assume that humans are perfectly rational or perfectly informed. Nor does it assume that humans operate in a sterile, frictionless environment in which every firm in an industry makes an identical product and trades it for the same price. As Adam Smith emphasized, market prices of goods and services emerge through exchange and are influenced by the institutions within which exchanges take place.

Smith's argument for the efficacy of the market is not based on unrealistic assumptions about its perfection—his view relies instead on the incentives and information that property, prices, profit, and loss provide to human actors. At its core are reasonable, choosing humans with foibles and fears, humans whose interactions are shaped by the sorts of messy, imperfect institutions that we have seen throughout history.[9]

Individuals—not organizations—act

James Buchanan was fond of reminding his students that neither governments nor corporations act; only individual people do. Simple though this idea seems, it is often forgotten. Because we speak of "Great Britain going to war" or of "Congress passing the Affordable Care Act" it is tempting to get sloppy and to forget that *individuals* in Great Britain and *individuals* in Congress made choices that led to these outcomes. Mainline economics embraces the proposition that acting individuals are the relevant unit of analysis. This idea is known as "methodological individualism."[10] It is important to note that methodological individualism is a scientific method of analysis; it is not an ideological commitment to individualism as personal or political philosophy.

Incentives matter

Acting individuals respond to incentives. And while we can never presume to know how every person will react in every situation, there are some regular patterns that seem to characterize human action. In particular, humans typically seek pleasure and avoid pain. Moreover, they make tradeoffs, weighing opportunities against one another. And they make these tradeoffs "at the margin" in the sense that they compare additional benefits of any activity with additional costs—including the additional opportunity cost of forgoing another activity.[11]

These simple ideas about incentives and tradeoffs yield the basic supply and demand models of economics and go a long way toward explaining an extraordinarily wide range of human behaviors. They tell us that when the cost of reckless driving is decreased—say, by laws requiring everyone to wear seatbelts—people will tend to "demand" more speed.[12] And they tell us that when ship captains who transport prisoners are paid for every live prisoner who disembarks rather than for every prisoner who boards—as happened after the British Crown took the advice of economists in 1793 and changed the way it paid captains shipping prisoners to Australia—the "supply" of live prisoners will rise.[13]

These ideas—that incentives matter, that demand curves slope downward, and that supply curves slope upward—should not be the final word in economic analysis. But they should almost certainly be at the beginning of any economic inquiry.[14]

Given the right institutions, individual actions will serve the common good

Methodological individualism disciplines economists and policymakers to think about micro-relationships such as the negotiation between a buyer and a seller or the coordinated plans of a network of social entrepreneurs. Given the ubiquity of macro-aggregates such as the unemployment rate and gross domestic product, these micro-foundations are easy to overlook. But a market—a society—is a complex combination of these innumerable micro-relationships.

The remarkable thing is that in market settings, these individual micro-behaviors often lead to desirable macro-outcomes. This was one of the main themes of Adam Smith's *Wealth of Nations*, and it is at the heart of his observation that "it is not from the benevolence of the butcher, the brewer, or the baker, that we expect our dinner, but from their regard to their own interest."[15] There are many reasons why markets might channel private self-interest toward the public good, and we discuss several in the pages that follow. For now, we can do no better than to quote Ronald Coase, who described this phenomenon in his famous 1959 paper on the Federal Communications Commission (which made the then-controversial case for deregulation of broadcast spectrum):

> This "novel theory" (novel with Adam Smith) is, of course, that the allocation of resources should be determined by the forces of the market rather than as a result of government decisions. Quite apart from the malallocations which are the result of political pressures, an administrative agency which attempts to perform the function normally carried out by the pricing mechanism operates under two handicaps. First of all, it lacks the precise monetary measure of benefit and

cost provided by the market. Second, it cannot, by the nature of things, be in possession of all the relevant information possessed by the managers of every business . . . to say nothing of the preferences of consumers.[16]

Property rights help us act better

Natural rights philosophers have long argued that the right to hold property is a fundamental human right.[17] Economists studying how different property rights regimes work in practice have found that the right to hold property *also* appears to be a fundamental prerequisite for human flourishing. A system of well-defined private property rights helps us live together peacefully, use our resources wisely, and plan for the future effectively.

The late economist Armen Alchian—who helped pioneer the economic study of property rights—defined a property right as "the exclusive authority to determine how a resource is used, whether that resource is owned by government or by individuals."[18] Note that the emphasis is not on the resource, but on how we treat it; it is a rule of behavior that determines what one may do with a certain resource.[19] In clarifying rules of resource usage, a system of well-defined property rights allows humans to peacefully coexist; in Alchian's terms, it "replace[s] competition by violence with competition by peaceful means."[20] A *private* property right, Alchian contended, has two additional attributes. It entails "the exclusive right to the services of the resource" and the right to "exchange the resource at mutually agreeable terms."[21]

Because private property owners bear the costs *and* reap the benefits of whatever decisions they make concerning their property, they are incentivized to use their property wisely. Thus, a system of well-defined private property rights also allows humans to achieve higher living standards by employing resources more efficiently. If, however, the right to access a particular resource is *not* exclusive, all those with access to it will tend to overexploit it, yielding a "tragedy of the commons."[22] We see this in overfished oceans, in overhunted elephant herds, and in many other commonly owned resources.[23] We also see the tragedy of the commons play out in city, state, and federal budgets in which numerous independent legislators are able to tap into a common fiscal resource.[24]

When private property rights are insecure, people tend to underinvest, fearing that they will never be able to enjoy the fruits of their investments. This starves an economy of capital, the lifeblood of production.

Insecure or incomplete private property rights also make it impossible to plan for the future. This was the crux of Austrian economist Ludwig von Mises's argument in the "socialist calculation debate." While many thinkers criticized socialism for its unrealistic goal of changing human nature, von Mises demonstrated that even if socialism succeeding in making humans less self-interested, it would fail because of economic planners' inability to rationally calculate the value of alternative uses of resources.[25] Without private ownership in the means of production, Mises reasoned, there would be no market for the means of production, and therefore no money prices for the means of production. And without money prices reflecting the relative scarcities of the means of production, economic planners would be unable to rationally calculate the alternative uses of the means of production (we elaborate on this point below in the section titled "Prices signal important information"). Tellingly, a spokesman for the Soviet foreign ministry understood this well. When he was asked whether the Soviet Union intended to make the whole world communist, he allegedly quipped that it hoped to make every country but New Zealand communist since it needed to get its prices from somewhere.[26]

The theoretical connection between private property rights and human flourishing is well supported by the data. Douglass North and political scientist Barry Weingast attribute the extraordinary advance in English living standards in the 18th century to the Glorious Revolution of 1688, which helped the government credibly commit to the protection of private property rights.[27] Other research documents the strong cross-country correlation between well-defined private property rights and economic development.[28]

Both policymakers and researchers should exercise humility

F. A. Hayek began his 1974 Nobel Prize lecture with an apology. Observing that the world economy was then caught in the grip of serious inflation, he noted that this condition was brought about "by policies which the majority of economists recommended." At the moment, he said, economists had "little cause for pride: as a profession we have made a mess of things."[29]

At the time of this writing, the financial crisis of 2008 and the Great Recession that followed are nearly a decade behind us. Yet we are still living with the aftereffects: slow growth,[30] diminished dynamism,[31] a collapse in economic freedom,[32] staggering debt,[33] and no end in sight for the federal government's implicit promise to rescue any firms it deems too big to fail.[34] As with the inflation of the 1970s, many of these problems can be traced back to the policy advice of economists. Given the potential for economic policy to cause great damage, the economist's oath ought to be that commonly ascribed to the physician: first, do no harm.

Much of what we have to say is a counsel in humility. It derives from several quarters. The Austrian school of economics teaches us that policy making authorities are unlikely to possess—in fact, are incapable of possessing—the requisite knowledge to direct the affairs of millions of their fellow humans. The public choice school shows us that even if central planners did possess the requisite knowledge to rule rightly, they are often tempted by perverse incentives to do the wrong thing. And new institutional scholars warn that even subtle changes in the rules can have far-reaching effects. Thus, as David Hume recommended in 1742, "in contriving any system of government, and fixing the several checks and controuls of the constitution, every man ought to be supposed a *knave.*"[35]

Or as Hayek averred, "If man is not to do more harm than good in his efforts to improve the social order," he must resist the temptation to see himself as a craftsman whose job it is to shape the handiwork of society. Instead, he must view himself as a gardener who cultivates growth "by providing the appropriate environment" in which humans may be free to make their own plans.[36]

3
MARKET
PROCESS
ECONOMICS[1]

"We are only beginning to understand on how
subtle a communication system the functioning
of an advanced industrial society is based—
a communications system which we call
the market and which turns out to be a
more efficient mechanism for digesting
dispersed information than any that man has
deliberately designed."

—*F. A. Hayek, Nobel Prize Lecture*[2]

"NOBODY," DECLARED ADAM SMITH, "ever saw a dog make
a fair and deliberate exchange of one bone for another with
another dog."[3] Humankind is one of the only types of animal
that exchanges with unrelated members of the species.[4] And
economics is fundamentally about exchange between choosing humans. Mainline economics emphasizes this fact, focusing on the exchange relationships that emerge in both market
and nonmarket settings.

Market exchange
is a process

A modern market economy, despite its unfathomable com-
plexity, is composed of a multitude of mutually beneficial
exchanges. The ancient Greek word *katallattein*, from which
English derives the term *catallaxy*, captures the essence of this
phenomenon. It describes exchange and the process by which
strangers are brought into friendship through exchange.[5]

The science that studies catallaxy in a market order falls under the domain of "catallactics." Catallactics focuses on the exchange relationships that emerge in the market, the bargaining that characterizes the exchange process, and the institutions within which exchange takes place. The mainline economic tradition emphasizes that the price system and the market economy are best understood as a *process of exchange* rather than as a static snapshot of the *outcome of exchange*—which is all one sees when looking at a supply and demand diagram on a piece of paper.[6]

The "facts" of the social sciences include what people believe and think

Physicists gained new insight into the workings of the universe when they abandoned the view that the natural world can be explained by divining the plans and purposes of inanimate objects, such as the sun and the moon. But unlike the physical sciences, the human sciences *begin* with the plans and purposes of individuals. In these sciences, if we ignore plans and purposes, we purge the science of human action of its subject matter. In the human sciences, the "facts" of the world are what the actors think and believe.[7]

The meaning that individuals place on things, practices, places, and people determines how they will orient themselves in making decisions. The goal of the science of human action is intelligibility, not prediction—we seek to understand human behavior, not predict it. Social scientists can gain some measure of intelligibility because as humans, we are what we study; we possess knowledge of our topic from within. In contrast, those who study the natural sciences cannot pursue a goal of intelligibility because they rely on knowledge from without. We can understand the plans and purposes of other human actors because we ourselves are human actors.

The classic thought experiment invoked to convey this essential difference between the sciences of human action and the physical sciences asks us to imagine a Martian observing the "data" at Grand Central Station in New York City. Our Martian could observe that when the little hand on the clock points to eight, there is a bustle of movement as bodies leave these boxes, and when the little hand hits five, there is a bustle of movement as bodies reenter the boxes and leave. The Martian may even develop a prediction about the little hand and the movement of bodies and boxes. But unless the Martian comes to understand the plans and purposes (commuting to and from work), his "scientific" understanding of the data from Grand Central Station would be limited. The sciences of human action are different from the natural sciences, and we impoverish the human sciences when we try to force them into the philosophical or scientific mold of the natural sciences.

Human action is based on subjective costs and subjective benefits

All economic phenomena are filtered through the human mind. Since the 1870s, economists have agreed that the value of a good is subjective. But, following the influential British economist Alfred Marshall, many have argued that the cost side of the equation is determined by objective conditions. Marshall believed that just as both blades of a pair of scissors cut a piece of paper, so subjective value and objective costs determine price. Marshall's insight that both blades matter was an important advance. But he failed to appreciate that costs, like values, are also subjective. This is because prices are themselves determined by the value that individuals assign to the alternative uses of scarce resources.[8] Both blades of the pair of scissors do indeed cut the paper, but the blade of supply—like the blade of demand—is determined by individuals' subjective valuations.

In deciding courses of action, one must choose; that is, one must pursue one path and not others. The focus on alternatives in choices leads to one of the defining concepts of mainline economics: opportunity cost.[9] The cost of any action is the value that one assigns to the highest-valued alternative that one must forgo in order to take the action. Since the forgone action is by definition never taken, when one decides, one weighs the expected benefits of an activity against the expected benefits of alternative activities.

Prices signal important information

Prices summarize the terms of exchange on the market. The price system signals relevant information (including the subjective values and opportunity costs of others) that helps market participants plan. As Hayek famously explained in his seminal essay "The Use of Knowledge in Society," pricing enables millions of independent people to "fit their plans in with those of others" without the need for any central coordinating authority or any coercion.[10] In so doing, the price mechanism helps us to realize mutual gains from exchange. In Hayek's famous example, when people notice that the price of tin has risen, they do not need to know whether the cause was an increase in demand for tin or a decrease in supply.[11] Either way, the increase in the price of tin leads consumers to economize on its use and encourages entrepreneurs to explore alternative, less costly methods of satisfying consumer desires. Market prices change quickly when underlying conditions change, leading people to adjust quickly.

It is, perhaps, easiest to appreciate the price system by examining what happens when it is not permitted to function. For example, in the 1960s and 1970s, the federal government imposed price controls on wellhead natural gas.[12] These controls forced the market price below the natural price that would have emerged in an open market, sending incorrect signals to both producers and consumers. For producers, the artificially low price acted like a "stop" sign, discouraging the sale of gas on the interstate market. For consumers, the artificially low price acted like a "go" sign, encouraging them to consume more natural gas. With consumers using more natural gas than producers were willing to bring to the market, many Midwestern cities experienced a series of natural gas shortages.

Competition is a process of entrepreneurial discovery

Many economists see competition as an end-state. In this supposed state, price equals marginal cost, and output is produced at the minimum point along the average cost curve. As University of Chicago economist Frank Knight often stressed, perfect competition means no competition.[13] By this he meant that competitive firms need not change their behavior in light of the actions of others; their behavior is preordained by the model (set price equal to marginal cost and produce the same thing everyone else is producing).

But in the real world of business, the term *competition* invokes an *activity*. If competition were a state of affairs, the entrepreneur would have no role. But because competition is an activity, the entrepreneur has a central role as the agent of change who prods and pulls markets in new directions. The competitive activity in the market is initiated by the lure of pure profit and disciplined by the penalty of loss.

As economist Joseph Schumpeter put it, the entrepreneur's role is to "reform or revolutionize the pattern of production."[14] The entrepreneur accomplishes this by developing new goods and new production methods, opening up new markets, exploiting previously unused resources, and developing new ways to organize firms.[15]

Entrepreneurs are alert to unrecognized opportunities for mutual gain. By seizing these opportunities, they earn profits, and the mutual learning from the discovery of gains from exchange moves the market to a more efficient allocation of resources.[16] In addition, the lure of profit continually prods entrepreneurs to seek innovations that increase productive capacity. For the entrepreneur who recognizes the opportunity, today's imperfections represent tomorrow's profits.[17]

Consider the "asymmetric information" problem in which sellers know more about the quality of their products than customers.[18] Though some see this as a significant imperfection in the market that can only be corrected through regulation, real world entrepreneurs have seen the imbalance as an opportunity to make money by correcting it. In the past, entrepreneurs have used bond posting, private certification, customer review systems such as Yelp, and third-party reviewers such as Zagat and Michelin to inform consumers and balance information asymmetry. More recently, a new generation of technologies has radically improved upon these systems, empowering consumers and enriching the entrepreneurs who developed them. The ride-sharing platform Uber, for example, permits customers to monitor drivers' routes in real time and prompts each and every customer to rate their driver. Uber monitors these ratings, rewards high performers by putting them first in the queue for new rides, and stops working with low performers. Customers, too, can see a driver's rating and can cancel a ride if they don't like what they see.[19] This communication of information is one reason why Uber has, in just a matter of years, displaced taxis in many major cities.

The price system and the market economy, therefore, are learning devices that guide individuals to discover mutual gains and to develop new and better ways to use scarce resources efficiently.[20]

Social outcomes are often the result of human action but not human design

For better or worse, many of the most important human practices are not the result of deliberate design but are the by-product of actions taken to achieve other goals. A student in the Midwest in January trying to get to class quickly while avoiding the cold may cut across the quad rather than walk the long way around. Cutting across the quad in the snow leaves footprints; as other students follow these, they make the path bigger. Although the students' goal is merely to get to class quickly and to avoid the cold weather, in the process they create a path in the snow that actually helps students who come later to achieve this goal more easily. (Some landscape architects wait to see where pedestrians have worn footpaths in the grass before they lay down walkways.) The "path in the snow" story is a simple example of how human societies, in the words of the Scottish Enlightenment political economist Adam Ferguson, "stumble upon establishments, which are indeed the result of human action, but not the execution of any human design."[21]

The market economy and its price system are examples of a similar process. People do not intend to create the complex array of exchanges and price signals that constitute a market economy. Their intention is simply to improve their own lot in life, but their behavior results in the market system. Money, law, language, science, and so on are all social phenomena that can trace their origins not to human design, but rather to people striving to achieve their own betterment, and in the process producing an outcome that benefits the public.

But not all spontaneous orders are good. In a pioneering piece that anticipated the techniques of "agent-based modeling," future Nobel laureate Thomas Schelling showed that even if individuals have a mild preference for living among their own kind (say, with 55 percent of the population sharing their ethnicity), they will nevertheless end up in extremely segregated neighborhoods, even though it is not the intent or desire of these individuals to live in such starkly segregated environments.[22]

Not all capital is created equal

Capital is the accumulated stock of assets—physical equipment, financial assets, and human knowhow—which helps us make and do more stuff. But how do producers know how to allocate their capital? Right now, people in Detroit, Stuttgart, and Tokyo are designing cars that will not be purchased for a decade. How do they know how to allocate resources to meet their goals?

The price system and profit and loss accounting guide production activities through time. Monetary calculation enables economic actors on the market to sort out from the numerous array of technologically feasible production projects those investments that are economically viable. Prices guide production; calculation enables coordination.[23]

Production is always for an uncertain future demand, and the production process requires different stages of investment ranging from the most remote (mining iron ore) to the most immediate (the car dealership). The values of all producer goods at every stage of production derive from the value consumers place on the final consumer product being produced.

Various production plans align goods at different stages of production into a capital structure that produces the final goods in, ideally, the most efficient manner. If capital goods were homogeneous, any capital good could be used to produce any final product consumers desired. If mistakes were made, the resources could be reallocated quickly, and with minimal cost, toward producing the more-desired final product.

But capital goods are not all the same. Nor are they perfectly substitutable. An auto plant can make cars, but not computer chips. The intricate alignment of different types of capital goods to produce various consumer goods and services is governed by price signals and the careful economic calculations of investors. If the price system is distorted, investors will make mistakes in aligning their capital goods. Once the error is revealed, economic actors will reshuffle their investments, but the adjustment can be painful, and in the meantime resources will be wasted.

The process of exchange works best when policy is predictable

One way to minimize the painful adjustments and wasteful misallocations that occur when price signals are distorted is for policymakers to adhere to policy rules that send clear signals about what policies the government intends to pursue. For this reason, many economists have called for rules-based, rather than discretion-based, policy making. This approach is akin to John Adams's appeal to "a government of laws, and not of men."[24]

As Hayek put it in *The Road to Serfdom*, consistent adherence to the rule of law means that "government in all its actions is bound by rules fixed and announced beforehand—rules which make it possible to foresee with fair certainty how the authority will use its coercive powers in given circumstances and to plan one's individual affairs on the basis of this knowledge."[25]

In the field of monetary policy—where central bankers often face extraordinary pressure to behave opportunistically—economists have long advocated adherence to rules.[26] In 1873, the British journalist and essayist Walter Bagehot suggested a widely acclaimed (though not always followed) rule for central banks during a financial crisis. Known as "Bagehot's dictum," it says that central banks should lend freely during a crisis but only to solvent firms, against good collateral, and at high rates of interest.[27]

A large number of economists, including Nobelists Milton Friedman, Finn Kydland, Edward Prescott, and Hayek himself, have argued that central bankers ought to be bound by rules when making monetary policy, rather than operating purely according to their own discretion.[28] Stanford University economist John Taylor has suggested that the central bank ought to commit to a rule that sets a target interest rate, and Milton Friedman wanted a rule that keeps the money supply at a constant rate of growth, while both Hayek and Mercatus economist Scott Sumner have called for rules targeting constant growth in nominal GDP.[29] Though the specific rule used to bind a central bank is hotly debated, the general proposition that rules are superior to discretion is widely accepted.[30] Mason economist and Mercatus scholar Lawrence H. White expressed this view in his testimony before the House Financial Services Subcommittee on Monetary Policy and Trade:

> Discretion in monetary policy and financial regulatory policy does not give us better results. It is today widely recognized that inflation is inadvertently fostered by the discretion of central banks, where "discretion" means the absence of precommitment to any fixed policy rule.[31]

Though the rules-based approach has gained its widest acceptance in the field of monetary policy, there is a case to be made for a rules-based approach to fiscal and regulatory policy as well.[32] Irresponsible fiscal policy can lead to macroeconomic imbalances and increased pressure on the monetary authority to inflate the money supply. Adam Smith referred to this as the "juggling trick" that governments engage in—the cycle of deficits, debt, debasement. A rule-bound policy regime is designed to curtail the juggling.[33]

APPLICATION 2:
UNLEASHING DYNAMIC COMPETITION

Few concepts command such universal respect among economists as competition. Unfortunately, what exactly is meant by competition is not so universally accepted. The textbook version of a competitive market—one in which a multiplicity of "price-taking" firms make identical products and set price equal to marginal cost—bears little resemblance to most real-world markets. Nor, as we note above, is this version of competition likely to accord with the way competition is used in everyday business conversation.

In real-world competition, entrepreneurs are alert to market conditions and act on their own volition to set price, quantity, and quality. These entrepreneurs often take actions that no economist could predict because the competitive process is itself a discovery process.[34] As economist Israel Kirzner has put it, the market process is "open-ended."[35] Mercatus senior research fellow Jerry Ellig demonstrated this point in his study of railroad deregulation.[36] While most economists, using given supply and demand conditions, had predicted that deregulation would lead to efficiency gains, Ellig shows that the gains far exceeded their expectations. This is because many of these economists had not considered the open-ended nature of competition and the dynamic competition that deregulation would unleash.

Mercatus senior research fellow Adam Thierer has shown that an open-ended discovery process requires "permissionless innovation."[37] Genuine, dynamic competition cannot happen unless the default policy presumes that new technologies and new business models are legal. Mercatus researchers have published in journal articles, taken to the airwaves, and written in the newspapers to stress this point as regulators across the country have moved to shut down "peer-production" ventures such as Uber, Lyft, and Airbnb.[38] Their message is getting through. "Permissionless innovation" has now entered the policy vernacular, and federal, state, and local policymakers in both the United States and Canada now regularly call on Mercatus experts for advice on how to protect dynamic competition in the emerging sharing economy.[39]

But entrepreneurship is not just about making money. Mercatus senior research scholar Emily Chamlee-Wright and senior research fellow Virgil Storr examined social entrepreneurship following the devastation of Hurricane Katrina.[40] Their work demonstrates the vital role that entrepreneurial discovery played in the effort to rebuild and overcome the unfortunate government-created barriers that often stood in the way of effective social action and experimentation. Working with Mercatus senior fellow Stefanie Haeffele-Balch and economist Laura Grube, Storr further examined commercial, political, and social entrepreneurship following Hurricanes Katrina and Sandy, arguing that local entrepreneurs were key drivers of disaster recovery, providing necessary goods and services, reconnecting social networks, and acting as focal points for return and recovery.[41]

This theme is also stressed by Mercatus senior affiliated scholar Steven Horwitz in his comparison of private and public post-Katrina relief efforts.[42] Horwitz shows that private organizations such as Wal-Mart were able to outperform public organizations such as the Federal Emergency Management Administration (FEMA). Wal-Mart arrived long before FEMA, had the supplies that communities needed, and helped restore order. As one local sheriff Harry Lee put it, "If [the] American government would have responded like Wal-Mart has responded, we wouldn't be in this crisis."[43] In some cases, Wal-Mart succeeded in spite of stiff federal resistance. For example, when the company brought in three trailers of water supplies, they were turned back by FEMA officials. Horwitz shows that these private groups—and, indeed, some effective public agencies, such as the Coast Guard—relied on decentralized systems that empowered local actors to make appropriate decisions based on the best information available.

APPLICATION 3:
THE GREAT RECESSION

In the crucible of the financial crisis of 2008, incoming White House Chief of Staff Rahm Emanuel asserted, "You never want a serious crisis to go to waste."[44] Many of his political opponents chided him for attempting to take advantage of the situation. But Emanuel's statement is consistent with a large body of research that finds that crises *do* often precipitate significant political and institutional change, sometimes for the better and sometimes for the worse.[45] Milton Friedman voiced a similar view in 1962 when he wrote, "Only a crisis— actual or perceived—produces real change."[46] When a crisis does occur, Friedman continued, "The actions that are taken depend on the ideas that are lying around. That, I believe, is our basic function: to develop alternatives to existing policies, to keep them alive and available until the politically impossible becomes the politically inevitable."

When the financial crisis struck, many pundits and policymakers viewed it as a clear sign of the unworkability of the free enterprise system and of the necessity for greater government control over private market interactions. For many policymakers, these were the "ideas lying around," and many of these ideas—the Troubled Asset Relief Program, the auto bailouts, the 2009 stimulus program, and the Dodd-Frank financial overhaul—made it into law.

Mercatus scholars, however, have worked to ensure that these are not the only ideas available. Their efforts to put the financial crisis and the public policy response in better context helped ward off some policy mistakes and have, hopefully, laid the groundwork for a better policy response when the next crisis comes.

Humans make mistakes, sometimes catastrophic ones. It is tempting—perhaps even morally satisfying—to blame a ruinous financial crisis and a deep recession on the greed, hubris, and stupidity of capitalists. But, as Mercatus affiliated senior scholar Russ Roberts puts it, "Greed, hubris, and stupidity are always with us."[47] The challenge is to explain why so many people made so many of the same mistakes at the same time. Public policy, with its ability to simultaneously alter the incentives of millions, may be one explanation for such systematic failure. Several pieces by Mercatus scholars help explain what happened during this period.

In *Gambling with Other People's Money*, Roberts explains how years of creditor rescues—including the bailout of Continental Illinois's creditors in 1984, the savings and loan rescues of the late 1980s and early 1990s, and the rescue of Mexico's private creditors in the mid-1990s—built an expectation that creditors would always be saved. This expectation encouraged firms to "leverage up" by financing their operations through debt rather than through equity.

The expectation of a bailout was particularly strong for the government-sponsored enterprises (GSEs), Fannie Mae and Freddie Mac. Privately owned, these firms were widely assumed to enjoy the backing of the federal government. This implicit (and ultimately, explicit) guarantee allowed them to borrow at one half of one percentage point less than their competitors, a significant competitive advantage.[48] This was not the GSEs' only privilege. As Mitchell explains in *The Pathology of Privilege*, Fannie Mae "also enjoyed a line of credit at the US Treasury, an exemption from state and local taxes, an exemption from Securities and Exchange Commission filing requirements, and lower capital requirements."[49] These favors came with strings attached. Roberts shows that policymakers systematically encouraged Fannie and Freddie to tilt their portfolios toward riskier investments.

In *Not What They Had in Mind*, Mercatus affiliated senior scholar Arnold Kling demonstrates that a key factor in the buildup of risk in the housing sector was "regulatory arbitrage."[50] Through this process, ever more complex regulations drove entrepreneurs to devise ever more ingenious methods of structuring their investments so as to minimize their regulatory capital requirements. This process systematically encouraged investment in mortgage-backed securities. It helped that ratings agencies—protected from competition thanks to their own regulatory privileges—failed to appreciate the growing risk and mistakenly gave these assets their highest ratings.[51]

In *The House That Uncle Sam Built*, Boettke and Horwitz show that the flames of the housing bubble were fanned by loose monetary policy, which encouraged the accumulation of labor and capital in housing, finance, and related industries.[52] When it became clear that these investments were not consistent with the underlying preferences of consumers, a painful adjustment became inevitable.

As the country plunged into its deepest recession in generations, policymakers grasped for a cure. Unfortunately, some of the most well-intentioned policy cures may have been more harmful than the disease. As we explain in an application in a following section, the massive fiscal stimulus of 2009, for example, may have been counterproductive because policymakers failed to take account of the public choice problems that always plague the implementation of policy.

To take another example, consider policy changes that appear to have reduced labor supply during the recession. In University of Chicago economist Casey Mulligan's studies of these changes,[53] he reports that both the federal government and the states altered eligibility rules for many programs, including Unemployment Insurance, Medicaid, and Supplemental Nutritional Assistance. These programs phase out as beneficiary income rises, creating what economists call "an implicit marginal tax rate" because beneficiaries lose benefits as their incomes rise. Mulligan finds that policy changes adopted during the recession caused this implicit marginal tax rate to rise from 40 percent to 48 percent for the median earner.[54] Applying standard estimates of the relationship between labor supply and marginal tax rates, Mulligan figures that perhaps half of the labor market depression during the Great Recession can be attributed to changes in these policies. In a subsequent paper for the Mercatus Center, Mulligan shows that the Affordable Care Act also raised both explicit and implicit marginal tax rates for many workers, especially female workers.[55]

Because of these efforts, when the next crisis hits, policymakers will have better ideas at hand.

4
INSTITUTIONS AND CULTURE

"In fact, a large part of what we think of as economic activity is designed to accomplish what high transaction costs would otherwise prevent or to reduce transaction costs so that individuals can freely negotiate and we can take advantage of that diffused knowledge of which Hayek has told us."

—*Ronald Coase, Nobel Prize Lecture*[1]

"INSTITUTIONS," ACCORDING TO Douglass North, "are the rules of the game in a society." They are the "humanly devised constraints that shape human interaction."[2] Institutions matter. Put the same set of people in two different institutional settings—say, one where property is held privately and another where it is held in common—and observe two very different sets of behavioral outcomes.

New institutional economics builds on neoclassical economics by embedding price theory in institutional and cultural context.[3] As we argue below, that context matters because transaction costs matter, and different underlying social structures can have a profound effect on transaction costs.

Transaction costs are real

Exchange—even mutually beneficial exchange—is costly. Individuals must find willing trade partners, haggle with each other over terms, and monitor one another to ensure they live up to their agreements. Together, these activities constitute the "transaction costs" of exchange.[4] They should not be confused with the *terms of trade*—the price the buyer agrees to pay the seller for a specified good or service. Instead, transaction costs are a burden that *both* buyers and sellers incur when they attempt to reach and enforce agreement on these terms. Transaction costs are often a problem. They gum up the process of exchange and make it more difficult for people to improve their condition through trade.

Ronald Coase first introduced the idea of transaction costs in an article from 1937 that has become a classic, "The Nature of the Firm." There, he argued that the "main reason why it is profitable to establish a firm would seem to be that there is a cost of using the price mechanism."[5] A firm reduces this cost by employing people in long-term contracts that take the place of separate agreements on each and every task that people in related lines of work might perform for one another.

Twenty-three years later, Coase again invoked transaction costs—but this time to explain how externalities might be handled through exchange.[6] Then, as now, externalities were a major concern of economists. An externality occurs when, in the course of exchange between buyers and sellers, third parties who have nothing to do with the exchange nevertheless bear either costs or benefits.

In 2013, some residents in Irwindale, California, complained that Huy Fong Foods' new sriracha hot sauce plant in town was making their eyes water and their throats sore.[7] The plant, they asserted, was not accounting for the cost that chili grinding and roasting imposes on those who happen to be downwind. The traditional solution to a problem like this, suggested by economist Arthur C. Pigou in 1920, is to tax polluters for whatever costs they impose on others. Taxation will make them recognize, or "internalize," the externality they impose on others and, if need be, change their operations.[8]

The "Pigouvian" solution is generally an improvement over command-and-control regulations because it allows producers with local knowledge to find the best way to mitigate costs. It is better, for example, than a regulation that mandates a particular technological solution that might become obsolete or inferior at a later date.

But there are problems with this approach. It requires policymakers to accurately measure the size of the externality cost, which is no easy task. Moreover, as Mason economist and Mercatus scholar John Nye has explained, it requires them to fully account for any *other* factors that might affect the quantity of the product produced or attempts to mitigate its harms, such as other taxes, subsidies, regulations, or bargains between the affected parties.[9] This makes finding the correct Pigouvian tax nearly impossible.

Coase suggested a different solution. It begins with the realization that an externality is "reciprocal." It isn't just about preventing A from inflicting harm on B, because "to avoid the harm to B would be to inflict harm on A."[10] If the sellers of delicious hot sauce are not allowed to make their product, they and their customers will be harmed. The owners and customers might even experience greater harm than those whose eyes and throats were filled with chili odor. "The problem," Coase asserted, "is to avoid the more serious harm."[11] To do this, however, we need to *measure* the harms; we need to know just how bothersome chili roasting is to neighbors, and how costly it would be to sriracha makers and their customers if they installed scrubbers, reduced output, relocated, or ceased operations.

Coase's insight was that in a world of minimal transaction costs and clearly delineated property rights, negotiation between sriracha makers and their neighbors would help us figure out the relevant harms. So long as either the producers or their neighbors have a clear property right to the air surrounding the operations ("an essential prelude to market transactions"), they will be able to negotiate with one another.[12] And, importantly, their negotiation will result in an agreement to avoid the greatest harm. Counterintuitively, Coase also showed that the parties will arrive at the exact same solution no matter how the courts assign the property right—that is, whether they declare that sriracha makers have the legal right to emit noxious fumes or whether neighbors have the legal right to compel sriracha makers to stop. Thus, Coase offered one more reason why property rights matter. (If you are wondering what happened to the sriracha plant, the two parties agreed to a solution before the dispute went to court. The plant is going to stay, but Huy Fong Foods agreed to install a new air filtration system. This is exactly the sort of agreement Coase said was possible).

Economist George Stigler dubbed Coase's insight the "Coase theorem."[13] Unfortunately, because Coase called attention to what would happen in a world of zero transaction costs, many have interpreted him to mean that *ours* was a world of zero transaction costs. In Coase's words, "Nothing could be further from the truth."[14] Instead, he highlighted transaction costs because he believed that in many cases they were significant and he thought it important to understand why.

Institutions matter because they determine the degree to which private property rights are clearly delineated and because they determine the size and scope of transaction costs. If a country's cultural and legal rules make it prohibitively expensive to use the price mechanism, its people will miss opportunities for mutually beneficial exchange. And they will be poorer for missing these opportunities. This is why, in the words of Nobel laureate Oliver Williamson, "New institutional economics is preoccupied with the origins, incidence, and ramifications of transaction costs."[15]

Institutions rule

In some ways it may seem unnatural to attribute differences in human behavior to differences in institutions. If we see a hot-headed friend become violent or an intemperate relative go into debt, it is rarely our first instinct to wonder how institutions may have shaped these decisions. In these cases, it seems more logical to attribute behavioral choices to the personalities and personal histories of these people. But if we look across the vast scope of time and place, we observe entire populations that seem systematically disposed toward violence or poverty. In many cases, these populations share the same history, the same geography, and even the same ancestry as other, less violent, more prosperous peoples.

When analyzing social outcomes at a society-wide level, institutional explanations often make more sense than personality-driven explanations. This was North's point in his Nobel lecture: "The organizations that come into existence will reflect the opportunities provided by the institutional matrix. That is, if the institutional framework rewards piracy then piratical organizations will come into existence; and if the institutional framework rewards productive activities then organizations—firms—will come into existence to engage in productive activities."[16] Or, as one paper puts it succinctly, "institutions rule."[17]

Indeed, economists have found that institutional differences around the world account for much of the observed disparity in the human condition. For example, a number of economists have found that in places such as Barbados, Cuba, and Saint-Domingue, early European settlers established institutions that gave far greater political and legal power to elites than to repressed—often racially segregated—underclasses.[18] In these places politically and legally privileged elites did all they could to retard creative destruction (see the discussion in the previous section on market process economics), fearing that it might jeopardize their own economic and political positions of power. Today, this legacy lives on in a legal and cultural heritage that remains hostile to entrepreneurship and creative destruction. The result, still evident several centuries later, is extreme poverty and inequality.

But it turns out that it is not only formal institutions that matter. As another paper puts it, "informal institutions rule" too.[19] Informal rules are private constraints that derive from customs, norms, and culture. Unlike formal institutions, informal institutions develop spontaneously. Formal and informal rules interact in important ways. Boettke, working with Mason and Mercatus economists Christopher Coyne and Peter Leeson, argues that successful economic development depends on whether or not formal rules are grounded in existing informal ones.[20]

Culture rules, too

Anyone who has dined out with a friend from another culture knows that there are different cultural mores about tipping. In fact, culture shapes, and is shaped by, every human exchange. This makes sense given that the market is, as Mason economist and Mercatus senior research fellow Virgil Storr notes, "a social space." The market is "where people form friendships, meet their husbands and wives, and connect with their parents, children, and siblings."[21] Recall that the word *catallaxy* connotes exchange and the process through which exchange brings strangers into friendship. This idea is captured by the meeting space in ancient Greek city-states called the agora, which served not only as a marketplace but as an area of social and political interaction. However, despite the deep relationship between exchange and culture, many economists ignore the market as a social phenomenon worthy of study.

When economists *have* attempted to incorporate culture into their studies of the market, they have often modeled it as a form of capital. This makes some sense given that, like capital, culture helps us produce other goods and services. But in many ways, as Storr argues in his 2013 book *Understanding the Culture of Markets*, neither capital nor culture is served well by the analogy. Unlike capital, culture is not a "stock" of resources acquired through prudence or thrift. Moreover, culture has important attributes that capital does not. Culture is best understood as a pattern of meanings shared by a group of people.[22] As Storr puts it, "Reality is processed through the lens of culture. As such, different cultural lenses can and do give rise to different conceptions of the good, different economic choices and so different economic outcomes."[23]

Cultural attitudes shape conceptions of what is and what is not appropriate to exchange (beer, life insurance, sex, blood, votes?), of who may exchange (elites, women, children?), and of how they may exchange (haggling, bartering?).

One important cultural norm is trust. It lubricates the wheels of commerce, allowing us to do business with people we've never met, expanding Adam Smith's "extent of the market."[24] Steve Knack, a senior economist at the World Bank, has gone so far as to claim, "If you take a broad enough definition of trust, then it would explain basically all the difference between the per capita income of the United States and Somalia."[25] In his work on anarchy, Leeson shows that, even in the absence of government, unrelated individuals often build trust in one another by adopting each other's cultural practices, closing the social distance that separates them and signaling their willingness to cooperate.[26]

Mercatus affiliated senior research fellow Omar Al-Ubaydli and his colleagues studied the determinants of trust in a laboratory setting and found that subjects primed to think about markets were more likely to trust strangers, perhaps because familiarity with markets teaches people that they can trust people they don't know.[27] This suggests a virtuous cycle: furthering progress depends on broadening the extent of the market, the extent of the market depends on trust, and trust can be nurtured by familiarity with markets.[28]

As we've previously noted, Deirdre McCloskey attributes the extraordinary rise of Great Britain in the 18th century to cultural changes that conferred newfound "dignity and liberty" on bourgeois pursuits.[29] She documents a remarkable transformation in cultural acceptance and, ultimately, celebration of the entrepreneurial spirit. But, of course, certain cultural norms can also be socially destructive. NYU economist William Baumol documents the consequences of cultural attitudes that celebrate "unproductive entrepreneurs" who come up with new and innovative ways to seek privileges rather than to create value for customers.[30]

Let freedom ring

Consider again Alchian's attributes of a private property right.[31] He says it entails the exclusive right to choose how a resource is to be used, the exclusive right to the resource's services, and the right to exchange that resource with others upon mutually agreeable terms. To varying degrees, governments abridge these rights. In Houston, there are very few zoning restrictions and—within the boundaries of tort, property, and contract law—one is allowed to use one's real property however one pleases. In most US cities, however, zoning regulations restrict the sorts of activities that may take place on one's real property. And in many markets, government wage and price controls make certain exchanges based on mutual agreement illegal.

As Alchian and others readily admit, it is not always possible to draw a bright line between my property and yours—

especially when certain activities on my property (burning leaves) interfere with your use of your property (smelling roses). In many ways it is helpful to think of a continuum of economic freedom along which property and other natural rights are more or less secure. At the economically free end of the spectrum, people are permitted to choose for themselves; they may voluntarily transact with whomever they wish, provided their actions do not infringe upon the like liberties of others.[32] At the other end of the spectrum, extensive regulations, burdensome taxes, and insecure private property rights limit choice and discourage mutually beneficial exchange.

Theory suggests that people will tend to prosper in places with greater economic freedom. In an effort to test this theory, economists—including those affiliated with the Mercatus Center—have developed several international and interstate measures of economic freedom.[33] These data support the theory. In a recent meta-analysis of 52 separate studies, economists Chris Doucouliagos and Mehmet Ali Ulubasoglu found that, "regardless of the sample of countries, the measure of economic freedom and the level of aggregation, there is a solid finding of a direct positive association between economic freedom and economic growth."[34] Of course, not all aspects of human well-being are captured by GDP growth. It is important, then, that papers also find that economic freedom correlates with other things that people value. A broad survey of all papers assessing the relationship between economic freedom and various measures of human well-being such as economic growth, living standards, life span, and happiness finds that among 198 empirical papers, over two-thirds found economic freedom correlates with "good" outcomes, and fewer than 4 percent found it is associated with "bad" outcomes.[35]

The right rules improve the way the game is played

While individual freedom may be philosophically and economically "ideal," it is by no means guaranteed that political orders will preserve freedom.[36] As Thomas Jefferson put it, "The natural progress of things is for liberty to yield, and government to gain ground."[37] Nevertheless, humanly devised constraints—institutions—can arrest this natural tendency. For example, while majoritarian democracy permits a majority to impose negative externalities on a minority (see the next section), a constitution that carefully limits the government to "limited and enumerated" powers can also limit the damage that a majority may do.[38]

Not all constitutional rules enhance efficiency or liberty, however. The original US Constitution infamously permitted chattel slavery (to put it in economic terms, it abrogated the most important property right of all, the right of self-ownership). And many legislative procedures help agenda-setters manipulate the outcome.[39]

A subfield of public choice and new institutional economics, known as "constitutional political economy," studies the rules of politics. It looks at how these rules operate and the processes by which they come into existence. As James Buchanan has put it, while economists routinely analyze human choice *within constraints*, "constitutional economics directs analytical attention to the *choice among constraints.*"[40]

As with all institutions, these political rules can be formal (such as the First Amendment prohibition against laws establishing religion or restricting its free exercise) or informal (such as the longstanding taboo against peacetime deficits).[41] They can also be the product of deliberate design (such as the US Constitution) or of centuries of unplanned evolution (such as the United Kingdom's constitutional law, made up of several documents and common law).[42] As Elinor Ostrom emphasized, these rules are often developed by institutional entrepreneurs, and sometimes their innovations don't conform to the simplified categories of "public" and "private." In her Nobel lecture she explains, "The classic assumptions about rational individuals facing a dichotomy of organizational forms and of goods hide the potentially productive efforts of individuals and groups to organize and solve social dilemmas such as the overharvesting of common-pool resources and the underprovision of local public goods."[43]

With the advent of constitutional political economy, there has been a revival of interest in constitutional design. Much of this was kicked off by two books. The first was Hayek's *Constitution of Liberty*, published in 1960. Two years later James Buchanan and his colleague Gordon Tullock—who, with Buchanan, was a founding father of public choice economics—published their seminal book, *The Calculus of Consent*.[44] Buchanan and Tullock showed, among other things, that representative republics whose legislative bodies have separate houses with members chosen in different ways will come closer to reflecting consensus than those that have a single house whose members are directly elected.[45]

A polycentric order is usually a good order

Though informal, bottom-up rules arise spontaneously, they often have their own logic. The chemist, economist, and philosopher Michael Polanyi termed the "mutual adjustment of a large number of centres" in a complex system a *polycentric order*.[46] While Polanyi applied the concept to the organization of scientific inquiry, a wide array of social phenomena fit his description. Think, for example, of the complex and overlapping web of systems that enforce property rights. Of course the state is one system that enforces these rights. But its agents, the police, are not always around. Nevertheless, theft is rare because other—often polycentric—orders prevent it. These include religious orders, workplace rules, cultural norms, and the mutual adjustments that attend all repeat dealings between people.[47] As Vincent Ostrom put it in an interview with Boettke and Mercatus senior research fellow Paul Dragos Aligica,

> We need not think of "government" or "governance" as something provided by states alone. Families, voluntary associations, villages, and other forms of human association all involve some form of self-government. Rather than looking only to states, we need to give much more attention to building the kinds of basic institutional structures that enable people to find ways of relating constructively to one another and of resolving problems in their daily lives.[48]

Vincent Ostrom, economist Charles Tiebout, and political scientist Robert Warren extended the notion of polycentricity to political economy in their study of metropolitan governance.[49] Reacting to the then-dominant "metropolitan reform" movement, they challenged the notion that each urban area should be governed by one unified government with limited or nonexistent separation of powers.[50] As Vincent Ostrom later described it, "We identified a polycentric political system as having many centers of decision making that were formally independent of each other."[51] The idea, he argued, is not unlike the separation of powers embodied in many constitutions.[52]

Contrasting it with monocentricity—in which all decisions flow through a single node—new institutional economists have emphasized a number of advantages of polycentricity.

Polycentric orders make better use of local knowledge, are more adaptable, and are more responsive to the demands of users—especially when users can opt in and out of different orders. Because decision makers in polycentric orders are typically local, they are able to craft solutions that better match the magnitudes of governance problems. Polycentric political systems also allow "public entrepreneurs" to experiment and take risks while containing exposure to risk. Finally, polycentricity leads to institutional diversity, with governance mechanisms that are calibrated to the preferences of groups, subgroups, and individuals.[53]

In her extensive studies of the effective management of common-pool resources, Elinor Ostrom found that polycentricity was key. For example, her work took her to California, where she studied water basins from which multiple parties could draw water. She found that not all water basins fell victim to the tragedy of the commons. Well-managed basins were "managed by a *polycentric set* of limited-purpose governmental enterprises whose governance includes active participation by private water companies and voluntary producer associations. This system is neither centrally owned, nor centrally regulated."[54]

Many problems that were once thought to require top-down government intervention are actually better resolved through bottom-up polycentric orders.

In its right form, federalism can preserve markets

"For most of the last 300 years," notes Barry Weingast, "the richest nation in the world has had a federal structure."[55] In the 16th and 17th centuries, the Netherlands claimed this title. In the 18th and 19th centuries it was England. And in the 20th century, it was the United States. A number of thinkers—including James Madison, F. A. Hayek, Charles Tiebout, and economist Wallace E. Oates—have identified federalism as an import market-preserving institutional mechanism.[56]

In his influential treatment of the subject, political scientist William Riker defined a federal system as one in which a hierarchy of overlapping autonomous governments coexist, with the spheres of autonomy being in some way institutionalized or self-enforcing.[57] Weingast identifies "market-preserving" federalism as a special species of federalism with three additional attributes.[58] First, the lower levels of government, rather than the central government, have primary responsibility for economic policy making. Second, there is a common market so that the lower levels cannot erect barriers to trade. And third, the lower levels of government face a hard budget constraint, meaning they cannot expect a bailout from the national government.

Though federalism and polycentricity are often confounded, Mason Professor and Mercatus scholar Richard E. Wagner and his coauthor, economist Akira Yokoyama, note that there are a number of important distinctions between the two concepts. Perhaps the most important of these is that while federalism denotes "a structure of government," polycentricity characterizes the spontaneous "process through which government entities operate within that structure."[59]

Perhaps the most celebrated consequence of market-preserving federalism is that it forces lower-level governments to compete with one another over capital, labor, and economic activity by developing institutional environments conducive to growth.[60] But just as private competition can be undermined by cartelization, so too can government competition. A number of authors contend that US federalism has become significantly less competitive over time. Many blame the federal government for facilitating this "cartelization" through various federal-state projects involving both funded and unfunded liabilities. In the words of Mason professor of law Michael Greve, this has turned the US Constitution "upside-down."[61]

APPLICATION 4:
INSTITUTIONS, NOT PERSONALITIES

Readers of *Politico*, *Roll Call*, or *The Hill* may be forgiven for thinking that politics is about personality. The implicit assumption in much political reporting is that if things are not working—if a program is losing money, an agency is plagued with corruption, or a policy is producing negative unintended consequences—then the problem is "bad leadership" and the solution is to put someone else in charge. Politicians challenging incumbent officeholders, of course, reinforce this perception. Indeed, every four years, a sizeable portion of idealistic first-time voters is courted by an attractive candidate offering nothing more than idealistic platitudes about change. The problem—as the classic rock band The Who put it—is that once in office, the new boss is usually the same as the old boss.

New institutional economics suggests that meaningful and lasting social change is likely to come from institutional change rather than from personnel change. And that is typically where Mercatus scholars have focused. Mercatus senior research fellows Jerry Ellig and Patrick A. McLaughlin and affiliated senior scholar John Morrall, for example, find that institutional factors, rather than the party of the president, are the most important determinants of quality in federal regulatory analyses. Different parties allow different agencies to get away with low-quality analysis, but the pattern of behavior is the same regardless of party.[62] In subsequent research, Ellig and Duke University economist Christopher Conover found that the George W. Bush and Obama administrations tolerated especially poor analyses for the first regulations implementing their signature policy priorities, homeland security and healthcare reform, respectively.[63]

In his study of the Base Realignment and Closure (BRAC) Commission, Mercatus senior research fellow Jerry Brito examined the characteristics of an institution that radically altered the incentives of public officials.[64] As the 1980s drew to a close and as the federal deficit continued to widen, many in Congress were looking for ways to reduce spending. Local military installations scattered throughout the country presented natural targets as top military brass were in agreement that many of these bases had outlived their strategic usefulness. The problem, however, was that bases had *not* outlived their political usefulness: they were a rich source of concentrated benefits for base employees in members' districts (see the discussion of concentrated benefits and diffused costs in the next section).

As Brito's analysis demonstrates, the BRAC Commission offered policymakers an incentive to side with taxpayers—a widely dispersed general interest—rather than with base employees—a highly concentrated special interest. Three factors made this possible. First, members were allowed to cast a conspicuous vote for the general interest by voting for a reduction in overall base spending. Second, the particular decision of where to cut spending was delegated to a panel of independent experts. Third, members were allowed to testify before these experts, imploring them not to cut spending in their own districts. This allowed members to escape some of the wrath of their hometown special interests and made them more likely to support the exercise in the first place. By all accounts, BRAC was successful. In its first iteration in 1988, 11 major bases were closed or realigned, and over the next few rounds, scores of additional bases were closed, so that by 1995, the Commission had closed 97 bases and realigned another 350.[65] Brito has suggested that the BRAC model might be applied to other areas of policy and has consulted with policymakers interested in making that a reality.

In her work on pensions, Mercatus senior research fellow Eileen Norcross draws attention to the perverse incentives that arise from misleading pension accounting practices.[66] Because public accounting guidelines induce government actuaries to use inappropriately high discount rates, these actuaries underestimate the true cost of pensions systems. This creates an externality problem: politicians select policies that confer benefits on current voters and current special interest groups—including public employees—while foisting the costs on future taxpayers. The problem is a manifestation of what the Italian economist Amilcare Puviani called "fiscal illusion."[67] When the costs of government are hidden or obscure, taxpayers and voters think government spending is less expensive than it actually is, and they demand more of it.

If the rules of the game, such as standard government accounting practices, produce bad results, the solution is not necessarily to select new leaders, but to select new rules. Indeed, because of the work of Norcross and other economists, there is growing pressure to change these rules. Several credit ratings agencies, the Congressional Budget Office, and prominent officials such as former Securities and Exchange commissioner Daniel Gallagher have now come out in favor of a market discount rate which will more accurately reflect the cost of these obligations.[68]

Prudent rule change, of course, requires an understanding of how rules actually operate. In their review of state-level institutions, Mitchell and Mercatus MA fellowship alum Nick Tuszynski look at sixteen different state-level institutions, including balanced budget rules, line-item vetoes, and term limits.[69] Some of these rules, such as strict balanced budget requirements, have been the subject of repeated study and have been routinely found to correlate with lower levels of per capita spending.[70] Others, such as item-reduction veto powers, have been largely neglected by researchers, even though those analyses that have been done find that they incentivize more prudent policy.[71] Finally, some rules, such as tax and expenditure limits, which are popular among fiscally conservative policymakers and advocates, either do not work as advertised or work only under certain circumstances.[72] Armed with a better understanding of the effects of these rules, policymakers in states across the country—including Illinois, Kentucky, and New York—are proposing institutional changes to improve the fiscal conditions of their states.

5
THE POLITICAL PROCESS

> "The relevant difference between markets and politics does not lie in the kinds of values/interests that persons pursue, but in the conditions under which they pursue their various interests."
>
> —*James Buchanan, Nobel Prize Lecture*[1]

GORDON TULLOCK, ALONG with James Buchanan, is often credited as a founding father of public choice economics. The late Mason professor and Mercatus scholar had a helpful allegory to describe the way economists thought of government before the advent of public choice.[2] He asks us to imagine a Roman singing contest. In this American Idol of antiquity, the emperor's guards have whittled the contestants down to two, each of whom must perform for the emperor, who will select the ultimate winner. The first contestant stands up and belts out a tune that is nice but has a few missed notes. Disgusted, the emperor orders his praetorian guards to kill the contestant and awards the honor to the second without ever hearing him sing. This, Tullock argues, is the way that economists approached public policy analysis before public choice. They "listened" to the market, identifying all of the ways it seemed to fail to live up to an idealized goal and then—without critically analyzing how government would perform in the market's stead—called for government intervention to take the place of market mechanisms.

Public choice economics listens to the second singer. It applies the tools of economics to political settings in order to understand how political outcomes are determined. This allows us to compare the actual performance of government with that of the market, neither of which is perfect. When it comes to government, this act of listening and observing does not come easily to many. This is because, as Christopher Coyne puts it in his study of state-led humanitarian aid, many discussions of government "focus on the moral responsibilities of governments" but "in focusing on the normative aspects of the issue—what governments *ought to do*—the positive aspects—what *can be done* . . . are often neglected."[3] The following elements are essential to the public choice toolkit.

Human nature is the same in and out of government

A consumer who selects peanut butter at the grocery store is also a voter who selects a president in the voting booth. This seems obvious. But a great deal of public policy is made with the implicit assumption that humans are stupid, nasty, or venal when they are in the supermarket or the boardroom but wise, angelic, and selfless when they walk into a voting booth or accept a civil service position. The incentives of public and private settings may indeed be very different. And in fact public choice researchers often find that incentives can be *worse* in public settings. But there is no reason to start the analysis with a romantic view of political activity. Indeed, James Buchanan defined public choice as "politics without romance."[4]

Humans are all rationally ignorant

No one is perfectly informed before he or she acts. That's because becoming informed is costly: it takes time, money, and effort to acquire information. In fact, it is completely rational to remain uninformed in those instances in which information will do us little good. That's why most of us know little about the physics of interstellar travel or the biology of the mongoose. When humans make important personal decisions—like getting married, buying a car, or accepting a job—they have a strong incentive to gather and process as much information about these actions (and the opportunities they preclude) as possible. But when humans make important political decisions—voting for a particular candidate or adorning their car with a political bumper sticker—they have little incentive to gather or process relevant information. This is due to the mathematical fact that one's vote or one's placement of a bumper sticker is extremely unlikely to change the outcome of an election. It is therefore rational to remain relatively ignorant about public policy and its implications.[5] This explains why most people are ignorant of basic political facts. Just one in three Americans, for example, can name his or her own representative in Congress.[6]

But as Mason professor of economics and Mercatus senior scholar Bryan Caplan has shown, it may be even worse. In his book *The Myth of the Rational Voter*, Caplan shows that when making political decisions it may make sense to indulge one's *irrational* prejudices.[7] This helps explain why people seem systematically disposed to vote for taller candidates,[8] for those who look like them, or for men who do not have "baby faces."[9]

There are externalities in politics, too

When humans act, their actions affect others and they occasionally fail to take these effects into account. Economists call this the externality problem and have typically identified it as one of the biggest "missed notes" of the market—necessitating government intervention.[10] Ironically, however, the process of government decision-making almost always entails significant externalities as well. Majorities select policies without accounting for the costs that spill over onto minorities; representatives buy local pork-barrel projects for their constituents and foist the costs onto the whole nation; regulators craft policies that impose costs on firms and their customers. Because of these externality problems, political outcomes almost certainly entail inefficiency.[11]

The political process concentrates benefits on the few and disperses costs across the many

In general, political benefits and costs are not randomly externalized. Typically there is a consistent pattern: benefits are concentrated on a small number of people while costs are dispersed over a large group. Consider sugar subsidies as an example. In recent years, federal loans to sugar producers (at below-market rates) have amounted to about $1.1 billion annually. Spread among 314 million Americans, this means that each American loans $3.50 each year to sugar producers. In 2013, only 17 firms received this largesse, and three of them received the bulk of it, about $200 million apiece.[12] This pattern is not unique to sugar subsidies. Almost any industry that benefits from protection receives a narrow benefit that is financed by a large number of taxpayers or consumers.

The late University of Maryland economist Mancur Olson attributed this phenomenon to what he called the collective action problem.[13] He observed that it is costly for individuals or groups to organize themselves in support of or in opposition to any public policy. Moreover, if a few people go to the trouble to get organized, others in their group (producers, consumers, taxpayers) can free-ride on their efforts. Somewhat paradoxically, smaller groups have an easier time overcoming these collective action problems than do larger ones, and this tends to make the smaller groups more powerful than the larger ones. Since consumers and taxpayers are almost always more numerous than producers, the theory predicts that producers will typically get the upper hand in the lobbying tug-of-war.[14]

When humans seek rent, resources are wasted

When one producer is the exclusive provider of a good or service, he or she is able to earn profit in excess of the normal, competitive market return. Economists refer to the above-normal profit of an exclusive producer as "economic rent."[15] This profit is above and beyond what would be necessary to induce producers to bring the good or service to market. Exclusivity can be natural; Michael Jordan naturally possessed a unique set of abilities that earned him a great deal of economic rent. But exclusivity can also be contrived; by law, only a limited number of taxis may operate in New York City. Because economic rents can be quite large, people are willing to go to great lengths to contrive exclusive privileges. And the expenditure of resources in an effort to contrive exclusive privileges is known as "rent-seeking."[16]

With its monopoly on the legitimate use of force, government can help firms contrive exclusivity in a number of ways: it can offer a legal monopoly; a subsidy; a loan guarantee; protection from foreign competition; a bailout; the *promise* of a bailout; favorable tax treatment; or a regulation that limits entry, mandates a product's purchase, or raises the costs of a firm's rivals.[17] Because government can help firms contrive exclusivity in these ways, it is common for firms to seek government's assistance. Firms will lobby. They will donate to campaigns and fund independent political advertisements. They will build unnecessary facilities that nevertheless employ a lot of people in important congressional districts. And they will market products with attributes that politicians desire rather than those with attributes that customers desire. All of this is potentially wasteful activity. It is the baggage of government-granted privilege. Estimates suggest that in the United States, annual rent-seeking costs are between 7 and 23 percent of gross national output.[18] In other words, rent-seeking acts as an extraordinarily large tax on our standard of living. Beyond this, however, privilege invites other problems, including diminished productivity and increased macroeconomic instability.[19]

Regulators get captured

The first federal regulatory body was the Interstate Commerce Commission (the Commission). Created in 1887 under pressure from various farm interests, policymakers hoped that the Commission would exercise its power to lower the prices that railroads charged for shipping produce to market. In time, however, railroad executives came to see the Commission as something that they could control. In 1892, US attorney general Richard Olney explained this point to his former employer, a railway man:

> The Commission . . . is, or can be made, of great use to the railroads. It satisfies the popular clamor for a government supervision of the railroads, at the same time that that supervision is almost entirely nominal. Further, the older such a commission gets to be, the more inclined it will be found to take the business and

railroad view of things. . . . The part of wisdom is not to destroy the Commission, but to utilize it.[20]

A century later, George Stigler drew attention to this phenomenon in a paper that would help win him the Nobel Prize in Economics. "As a rule," Stigler wrote, "regulation is acquired by the industry and is designed and operated primarily for its benefit."[21] Stigler's theory, which came to be known as "regulatory capture," is precisely what Olson and others would predict: given the fact that firms are less numerous than their customers, they will tend to have the upper hand in organizing and influencing their regulators.[22] Moreover, given the highly technical nature of many regulated processes, agencies have little choice but to rely on firms for their knowledge and expertise. In many cases, agencies employ former industry employees to help them craft their rules.[23] At the same time, officials leaving regulatory or political bodies can command large salaries if they go to work for the firms they once oversaw—especially if they still have connections in their old office.[24] This phenomenon, known as the "revolving door," means that public officials eyeing a future private job will tend to be more sympathetic to the industry's "view of things."[25]

Politics makes strange bedfellows out of "bootleggers" and "Baptists"

When a firm "captures" a regulatory body or seeks rent from a politician, it is often aided and abetted by other interest groups, many of which have pure (or at least less nefarious) motives. For example, though railway men eventually came to dominate the Interstate Commerce Commission, it was originally created at the behest of farmers seeking relief from high shipping costs. Regulatory economist Bruce Yandle called this the "bootlegger and Baptist" theory of regulation.[26] Drawing on the example of blue laws that forbid alcohol sales on Sundays in some counties, Yandle noted that these laws are often promoted by two strange bedfellows. Baptists support the laws because they wish to limit the consumption of alcohol on the Lord's Day. But bootleggers, who already circumvent the law, also support such bans because they value having the market all to themselves one day a week.

Bootlegger and Baptist coalitions are quite common. As Congress debated the Affordable Care Act, advocates for the uninsured played the part of the Baptists, while insurance companies that thought they stood to gain from the individual mandate played the part of the bootleggers. A California lawmaker recently played the part of both bootlegger and Baptist. State Senator Leland Yee has long been known for promoting strict gun control. In 2013 he sponsored one of the nation's most restrictive gun control bills (it was eventually vetoed by Governor Jerry Brown). One year later, the FBI arrested Yee for arms trafficking. In exchange for campaign donations, the lawmaker offered to connect an undercover agent with an international arms dealer.[27]

Agenda setters may be able to determine the outcome

Other things being equal, if you prefer whiskey to beer and beer to water, it stands to reason that you prefer whiskey to water.[28] This is known as "transitive preference ordering," and the vast majority of humans over age 13 exhibit strongly transitive preference orderings.[29] A funny thing about the democratic process, however, is that even if every single voter has transitive preference orderings, the electorate as a whole can exhibit *intransitive* orderings.[30] In other words, if a group of diners were to vote on an after-dinner drink, it is entirely possible that—without anyone changing their mind—in three separate elections, whiskey could beat beer, beer could beat water, and water could beat whiskey. This is known as a "voting cycle."[31]

There are a number of problems with voting cycles.[32] For one thing, they belie the notion—popular in some quarters—that elections somehow resolve differences and help political communities attain understanding of higher truths.[33] The reality is that the electoral outcome can, in some instances, be random, depending on the order in which votes are taken. In this sense, elections do not resolve differences; they just disguise them. Another problem with voting cycles is that they invite manipulation. If the outcome depends on the order in which votes are taken, then a committee chairman, the Speaker of the House, or anyone else with the power to set the agenda can manipulate the process to ensure his or her most-preferred outcome wins.[34] This is one reason why leadership positions in Congress are so coveted.

Politics is about exchange

Earlier, we noted Adam Smith's observation that humans possess "a natural propensity to truck, barter, and exchange one thing for another."[35] James Buchanan and other public choice economists emphasize that this propensity extends beyond the supermarket and into political settings, where policies are "purchased" through the exchange of votes, endorsements, campaign dollars, and (many) words.[36]

In one sense, this is a decidedly unromantic view of politics. As Buchanan put it, it means that political engagement is *not* a "common search for the good, the true, and the beautiful."[37] But Buchanan also emphasized that the view of politics as exchange is not entirely pessimistic, either.

In this, Buchanan was perhaps more optimistic about government than many of his public choice colleagues. "Individuals acquiesce in the coercion of the state, of politics," he wrote, "only if the ultimate constitutional 'exchange' furthers their interests."[38] In other words, citizens' relationships with their government ought to be positive-sum over the long run.

APPLICATION 5:
GIVING VOICE TO DIFFUSE INTERESTS

Though Olson's "logic of collective action" suggests that the political scales will tend to tilt toward small, highly organized interests, his theory does not rule out the influence of other factors.[39] It does not, for example, preclude the possibility that academic ideas can influence the climate of opinion, raising the political costs of bad policy and lowering the costs of good policy.[40] Indeed, much Mercatus research speaks for the widely diffused and unorganized interests that might otherwise bear the costs of bad policy in silence.

The Mercatus Center's decades-long efforts to achieve better regulatory impact analysis is one example.[41] A comprehensive and well-informed regulatory impact analysis begins with an assessment of whether a problem is systematic and merits government intervention. Next, the analysis requires that analysts develop alternative solutions that are linked to the cause of the problem, including the alternative of not regulating. Finally, it requires that regulators assess the benefits and costs of these alternative courses of action.[42] As in all public policy decisions, benefit-cost analysis requires a healthy dose of humility. Both benefits and costs are subjective and are heterogeneous across individuals.[43] Luckily for economists, market prices shed light on these subjective valuations so analysts can often use market prices to approximate the values people place on benefits and costs. Absent a concerted effort to measure these subjective benefits and costs, rule makers hear only from the concentrated interests that stand to gain from regulations—but not from the diffuse consumers and taxpayers who may pay for the regulations.

In recent years, Mercatus scholars have developed some creative tools that allow researchers to get a better handle on the scope and effect of federal regulations. Mercatus senior research fellows Omar Al-Ubaydli and Patrick A. McLaughlin wrote computer algorithms that classify all parts of the *Code of Federal Regulations* according to the industries that each regulation targets.[44] Additionally, their algorithms note the use of restrictions—words like *shall*, *must*, or *may not*, which create binding legal obligations—in these same regulations. These measures permit researchers to compare the extent of regulation across industries and over time. Their efforts permit, for the first time, detailed and industry-specific research on the effect of regulation on industry performance,[45] entrepreneurship,[46] and dynamism.[47]

In many cases, Mercatus research has saved diffuse interests substantial sums of money. Consider state and local barriers to entry in cable television markets. Because local governments have historically refused to grant new franchises to cable operators, incumbent firms have enjoyed some degree of monopoly pricing power, allowing them to charge higher prices while offering lower-quality service. In 2005, Mercatus senior research fellows Jerry Brito and Jerry Ellig began studying the issue, eventually filing a comment in the Federal Communication Commission's (FCC) proceedings and writing a law review article.[48] They also delivered multiple talks on Capitol Hill and testified before both the California State Legislature and the US Senate Committee on Commerce, Science, and Transportation. In December of 2006, the FCC ruled on the issue, adopting many of Brito and Ellig's recommendations and citing their public interest comment nine times. The ruling makes it harder for local governments to block entry into the cable television market, providing widely dispersed customers up to $7 billion in cost savings and quality improvements.

Or consider the Export-Import Bank of the United States (Ex-Im Bank). An independent federal agency that helps finance export deals, the Ex-Im Bank is a classic example of Olson's logic. Its benefits redound to a select group of exporters, a handful of which receive the bulk of its assistance.[49] But its costs are borne by a large and diffuse group of taxpayers, borrowers, and consumers.[50] Though the individuals who compose these groups have little incentive to get organized and make their voices heard, Mercatus researchers have given them a voice. In a series of working papers, op-eds, letters to the editor, charts, videos, blog posts, media appearances, congressional briefings, and congressional testimonies, Mercatus researchers—especially senior research fellow Veronique de Rugy—have indefatigably explained the economics of the Ex-Im Bank, drawing much-needed attention to the fact that its costs are real. In the summer of 2014, for example, Mercatus published 51 distinct op-eds and letters to the editor on the topic.[51]

Thanks to the work of de Rugy and others, the agency's reauthorization in 2015 was more controversial than at any point in its 80-year history. Moreover, in order to get it passed, floor leaders tied the Ex-Im Bank vote to a continuing resolution that most members felt compelled to support, lest they be blamed for a government shutdown. The Ex-Im Bank was only reauthorized for nine months (the shortest reauthorization in its history), and at the time of this writing, its fate remains uncertain.

APPLICATION 6:
THE STIMULUS DEBATE

Is fiscal stimulus effective? The answer turns, in part, on macro-economic debates concerning how governments and households react to temporary cash infusions. Milton Friedman predicted that households and governments would likely use such infusions either to pay down debt or to smooth consumption over the long run, thus blunting the stimulative effect.[52] Indeed, in his study of the massive 2009 fiscal stimulus, John Taylor found that households and govern-ments did just that.[53]

But the effectiveness of fiscal stimulus also depends on politics. After all, political actors—not academic economists—determine when, where, and how stimulus is implemented. Near the end of his life, Lord Keynes himself expressed doubt that the political process was capable of administering stimulus in a responsible way. In 1942, he wrote:

> Organised public works, at home and abroad, may be the right cure for a chronic tendency to a deficiency of effective demand. But they are not capable of sufficiently rapid organisation (and above all they cannot be reversed or undone at a later date), to be the most serviceable instrument for the prevention of the trade cycle.[54]

More recently, Keynesian economist Lawrence Summers warned that fiscal stimulus "can be counterproductive if it is not timely, targeted, and temporary."[55] Note that each of these requirements depends on implementation, and therefore on the political process. Consider each in turn.

Is stimulus timely? In the working paper "Would More Infrastruc-ture Spending Stimulate the Economy?," Mitchell and de Rugy explored this question. Highlighting the fact that infrastructure projects involve planning, bidding, contracting, construction, and evaluation, they note, "By nature, infrastructure spending fails to be timely."[56] Though it should be well known that infrastructure proj-ects simply cannot be implemented quickly and are therefore not a good candidate for stimulus spending, public choice pressures give policymakers a strong incentive to spend on conspicuous permanent projects. Thus, approximately 45 percent of the American Recovery and Reinvestment Act's (ARRA) funding was allocated to infrastructure.[57] This explains why 28 months after it passed, only 62 percent of ARRA funds had been spent.[58]

Is stimulus targeted? A number of Mercatus studies have explored this question. In "Stimulus Facts," de Rugy found that ARRA funding had no statistically significant relationship with regional unemployment rates, suggesting it failed to target those areas worst hit by the recession.[59] She was the first to document this fact, and others soon corroborated her finding.[60] There is evidence that ARRA missed its target at the micro level as well. Mercatus researchers Garett Jones and Daniel Rothschild discovered that most of those newly hired through ARRA had not been previously unemployed.[61] In their first-of-its-kind study, Jones and Rothschild sent research teams across the country to interview stimulus recipients about their experiences. They found that just 42.1 percent of those workers hired at ARRA-receiving organizations were unemployed at the time they were hired.[62] Real-world stimulus—in contrast with the idealized stimulus imagined by Keynesian economists—does not employ idle resources.

Is stimulus temporary? Public choice theory predicts that each government spending program will tend to create its own constituency of concentrated interests ready and organized to fight for its continuance. In a 2010 Mercatus working paper, economists Russell Sobel and George Crowley found that when the federal government transfers resources to the states, the states tend to increase their own taxes in order to maintain funding levels, even after federal funding is discontinued.[63] This finding suggests that Lord Keynes was, indeed, right to worry that "above all," public works projects "cannot be reversed or undone at a later date."[64]

Finally, in recent research, economist Jason Taylor and Mercatus's Andrea Castillo survey the historical record dating back to the 1930s. They conclude that it is a "false premise" that "expansions of government size and scope during times of crisis are timely, targeted, and temporary."[65]

The debate about fiscal stimulus has often turned on narrow macroeconomic questions, such as the size of the fiscal multiplier (a measure of how government purchases affect the economy). This is an important question and, indeed, Mercatus research has contributed some answers to it.[66] But knowing that because of public choice processes, real-world stimulus is neither timely, targeted, nor temporary, is at least as important as knowing the size of the multiplier.[67]

6
A LIBERAL PROGRAM THAT APPEALS TO THE IMAGINATION

> "Historically, a recurrent theme in economics is that the values to which people respond are not confined to those one would expect based on the narrowly defined canons of rationality."
>
> —*Vernon Smith, Nobel Prize Lecture*[1]

IN THE SPRING of 1949, in the *University of Chicago Law Review*, F. A. Hayek issued a challenge to the classical liberal scholars and thought leaders of his time. He called on them to "make the building of a free society once more an intellectual adventure, a deed of courage."[2] They must "offer a new liberal program which appeals to the imagination" and cultivate an intellectual movement that embraces a form of "liberal radicalism" that does not shy away from taking on either the politically powerful or the intellectually complacent. In short, their challenge was to "make the philosophic foundations of a free society once more a living intellectual issue, and its implementation a task which challenges the ingenuity and imagination of our liveliest minds."

A younger generation of scholars—including future Nobel Prize winners James Buchanan, Ronald Coase, Douglass North, Vernon Smith, and Elinor Ostrom—took up Hayek's challenge in various ways. Their joint labors in the subsequent decades of the 20th century yielded new insights in political economy, dynamic and entrepreneurial market processes, and institutions of both free and unfree societies. They also extended and enhanced old understandings that had long been in the mainline of economic thinking. In so doing, they paved the way forward for a robust political economy in theory and in practice for the 21st century.

At the Mercatus Center at George Mason University we consider the ideas of these social scientists and their colleagues our "toolkit." Our aim is to put these tools to work to build a better community. It is to answer the question that James Buchanan asked at the end of his own Nobel Prize lecture: "How can we live together in peace, prosperity, and harmony, while retaining our liberties as autonomous individuals who can, and must, create our own values?"[3] Through original research, graduate education, public policy analysis, media appearances, and outreach efforts, we aim to bridge the gap between cutting-edge academic ideas and the pressing problems of the real world. In these pages, we have described the important elements of this toolkit. Our discussion has also included a number of applied case studies that examine how these tools have been employed by Mercatus scholars to help realize Hayek's vision of a freer, more prosperous society.

When Hayek issued his challenge to make the building of a free society a deed of intellectual courage, his was a lonely voice. At that time, in the middle of the 20th century, central planning and the neo-Keynesian approach to economics and public policy reigned supreme. But by the late 1970s, the weaknesses of these approaches had begun to show themselves. It was widely agreed by observers on both the political left and right that regulations on price, entry, and technology had generally been wasteful and anticompetitive.[4] The Nixon administration's price controls had produced painful and embarrassing shortages, especially in energy and food markets. The Federal Reserve's expansion of the monetary base by nearly 25 percent between 1974 and 1976 had led to double-digit inflation.[5] And contrary to Keynesian modeling, this inflation coincided with stubbornly high unemployment rates, necessitating a new word to describe the phenomenon—*stagflation*.

As these problems mounted, several disparate and occasionally antagonistic schools of thought had begun to poke holes in the Keynesian intellectual edifice. In 1979, James Buchanan was a professor of economics at Virginia Polytechnic Institute. There, in the foothills of the Blue Ridge Mountains, Buchanan penned a tribute to his friend F. A. Hayek. In it, he argued that these new schools of thought could be strengthened through intellectual exchange: "The diverse approaches of intersecting 'schools' must be the bases for conciliation, not conflict. We must marry the property-rights, law-and-economics, public-choice, Austrian-subjectivist approaches."[6]

In this, Buchanan aspired to recreate the sort of intellectual environment that had prevailed at the London School of Economics (LSE) in the 1930s. Hayek had spoken approvingly of that environment, noting that economist Lionel Robbins's LSE seminar had aimed "at the synthesis of the various still-prevailing schools" and that this synthesis forged a new appreciation of classical liberalism.[7] In 1983, four years after he had called for a conciliation of the various schools of thought, Buchanan and his colleagues decamped for George Mason University, bringing the Center for the Study of Public Choice with them. There, they joined the Austrian-inspired Center for the Study of Market Processes that had been established at Mason a few years earlier and would eventually become the Mercatus Center. Three years later, Buchanan's contributions to economics were recognized with the Nobel Memorial Prize in Economic Sciences.

Over the decades that followed, the vision that Buchanan laid out in that 1979 tribute was realized at George Mason. The property rights, law and economics, public choice, and Austrian-subjectivist approaches to economic analysis were brought together into an exchange approach to political economy. The wedding of these disparate schools of thought produced a new brand of economics, which some have dubbed "Masonomics."[8]

Buchanan and his colleagues arrived shortly after the reconstituted economics department at Mason had established its PhD program. In both their research and their graduate education, they built a program focused on microeconomics and political economy. From the beginning, their work was grounded in the Austrian and public choice schools of economics and political economy. One of the first public lectures given at this newly formed PhD program was by Hayek, and he dealt with the ideas that would eventually constitute his final book, *The Fatal Conceit*.[9]

Another important step in the development of Masonomics came when, in 1986, Henry Manne, one of the founders of the law and economics discipline, became the dean of the George Mason University Law School. Over the next decade Manne would develop the school into one of the world's leading research and educational centers for law and economics. The economics department has close ties with the law school; several professors have dual appointments in both programs, and—quite uniquely—the economics program offers a law and economics field as part of its graduate curriculum.

The law and economics pioneer Ronald Coase (a one-time colleague of Buchanan and Gordon Tullock at the University of Virginia) had a deep influence on both the economics department and the law school. In the economics department, for example, what might be called the often-neglected branch of Chicago price theory permeated the core courses of the graduate program.[10] This perspective, which is best exemplified by the work of Armen Alchian, James Buchanan, and Ronald Coase, draws on the "old Chicago" tradition that places economic exchange and the institutions within which exchange occurs at the center of analysis.[11] But the neglected branch of Chicago price theory extends the older tradition by applying the logic of choice to the discovery of *new institutional arrangements* and by stressing the importance of *institutional entrepreneurs* who bring about these new arrangements.[12]

Because of this institutional focus, Douglass North's new institutional analysis and research into European and US economic history also influenced the graduate curriculum.[13] In the early 2000s, this relationship with North's ideas grew stronger as the Mercatus Center began working with him on a series of book manuscript seminars. Mercatus has continued to offer these manuscript seminars for other authors to this day.[14] Vincent and Elinor Ostrom—both former presidents of the Public Choice Society—also had a strong formal and informal influence on the intellectual environment at Mason.[15] And finally, Vernon Smith, who joined the Mason faculty with his research team in 2001, had a marked impact. Smith is best known for his innovation of experimental economics, but he is a wide-ranging scholar whose ideas have traversed property rights, law and economics, public choice, and market process economics. The year after his arrival at Mason, Smith was awarded the Nobel Prize in Economics. In his Nobel Prize lecture, Smith's intellectual affinity with Hayek, Buchanan, Coase, North, and the Ostroms was clear.[16]

As Buchanan predicted, the wedding of these disparate schools of thought yielded an intellectual whole that is stronger than the sum of its parts, offering further evidence of the mutual gain through exchange. "Nobody," as Hayek once put it, "can be a great economist who is only an economist."[17]

By synthesizing and extending the insights of Hayek, Buchanan, Coase, North, Smith, and the Ostroms, Mason economists and social scientists aim not only to address the cutting edge of academic discourse but to bridge the gap between this academic discourse and real-world problems. To that end, Mason economists have become active public intellectuals. George Mason University economists have adopted the motto that we must "dare to be different," as James Buchanan stressed when he and his colleagues moved to the university, and it is a stylistic hallmark of the economists working and training in the environment to do "economics with attitude."[18]

Through persistent and consistent application of economic reasoning to the most pressing issues in public policy, Mason social scientists contribute to the cutting edge of science. These scholars are committed to communicating the insights of mainline economics not only to their scientific peers in journal articles and academic books but to the world at large. From the syndicated columns of Walter Williams—which reach audiences in about 140 newspapers nationwide—to the bestselling books and popular blogs of Mercatus general director Tyler Cowen, George Mason economists reach far beyond the ivory tower. They engage college students through textbooks, autodidacts through massive open online courses; policymakers through Capitol Hill briefings and testimony; and the general public through blogs, op-eds, social media, viral videos, public lectures, and radio and TV interviews. In all of this, Mason researchers are aided by Mercatus's world-class media and outreach teams who see to it that their work has a wide and influential audience. Mercatus itself began as a small research group in the early 1980s that did little more than support a few graduate students and has grown to a major research, education, and outreach center with broad influence on both academic and policy debates.

James Buchanan wanted a marriage between the property rights, law and economics, public choice, and Austrian schools of economic thought. For the past 35 years, economists, legal scholars and other social scientists have been synthesizing and extending these research programs. Thanks to their work, Buchanan's dream has largely been realized.

What has this union produced? First and foremost, it has yielded better understanding. Because of these efforts, we now have a deeper knowledge of human exchange and entrepreneurship, of political bargaining and agenda setting, and of the social and political institutions within which exchange takes place. We also have a stronger case for human freedom—including economic freedom. This case is not founded in faith nor in naïve optimism that the market will always work perfectly. It is based neither on a model of man that assumes we are all super-rational optimizers nor that we operate in frictionless environments in which institutions are perfect (despite their mathematical elegance, such assumptions are often unrealistic).[19] Instead, the case is grounded in what we have called the mainline economic tradition that dates back to Adam Smith.

James Buchanan sought to rediscover this mainline of political economy and contrasted it with the then dominant vision of the discipline that viewed economics as a tool to be employed by policy experts interested in countering microeconomic inefficiency, macroeconomic imbalance, and social injustice. Buchanan argued instead that political economists must focus, as we have discussed, on the rules level of analysis. As Buchanan put it,

> Political economists stress the technical economic principles that one must understand in order to assess alternative arrangements for promoting peaceful cooperation and productive specialization among free men. Yet political economists go further and frankly try to bring out into the open the philosophical issues that necessarily underlie all discussions of the appropriate functions of government and all proposed economic policy measures.[20]

For Buchanan—like Hayek and Smith and many others—this frank discussion of philosophical issues led to a deep appreciation for human freedom and to a conscious effort to cultivate cultural respect for that freedom.[21]

This case for freedom is also eminently practical. It rests on a series of observations that in the real world, (1) competition is an open-ended process of entrepreneurial discovery, (2) prices guide this discovery process and allow disparate individuals to coordinate their plans, (3) imperfections in the process create profit opportunities for entrepreneurs able to correct these problems, (4) interference with mutually beneficial exchange often creates undesirable unintended effects, (5) unproductive entrepreneurs can capture the political process and exploit it for their own gain at the expense of the diffuse and the politically unorganized, and (6) good institutions guide self-interested individuals (as if by an invisible hand) to promote the interests of society while bad institutions guide them to cause great human suffering.

Through our research and educational efforts at the Mercatus Center, we aim to make this case to our colleagues in academia, to the public, and to change agents who shape policies and institutions. In short, we hope to develop a workable liberal program that appeals to the imagination.

FURTHER READING

The Core Themes of Mainline Economics

Barry, Norman. "The Tradition of Spontaneous Order: A Bibliographical Essay." *Literature of Liberty: A Review of Contemporary Liberal Thought* 5, no. 2 (1982): 7–58.

Boettke, Peter J. *Living Economics: Yesterday, Today, and Tomorrow.* Oakland, CA: Independent Institute, 2012.

Boettke, Peter J., Stefanie Haeffele-Balch, and Virgil Henry Storr, eds. *Mainline Economics: Six Nobel Lectures in the Tradition of Adam Smith.* Arlington, VA: Mercatus Center at George Mason University, 2016.

Buchanan, James M. "What Should Economists Do?" *Southern Economic Journal* 30, no. 3 (1964): 213–22.

Smith, Adam. *The Theory of Moral Sentiments.* Indianapolis: Liberty Fund, 1984. First published 1759.

Smith, Adam. *The Wealth of Nations.* Indianapolis: Liberty Fund, 1981. First published 1776.

White, Lawrence H. *Clash of Economic Ideas: The Great Policy Debates and Experiments of the Last Hundred Years.* Cambridge: Cambridge University Press, 2012.

Market Process Economics

Boettke, Peter J., and Christopher J. Coyne, eds. *The Oxford Handbook of Austrian Economics.* Oxford: Oxford University Press, 2015.

Hayek, F. A. *Individualism and Economic Order.* 1948. Reprint, Chicago: University of Chicago Press, 1996.

Hayek, F. A. *Law, Legislation and Liberty, Volumes 1 and 2.* Chicago: University of Chicago Press, 1978.

Kirzner, Israel M. *Competition and Entrepreneurship.* Vol. 4 of *The Collected Works of Israel M. Kirzner.* Indianapolis: Liberty Fund, 2013. Paperback version published 1978 by University of Chicago Press.

Kirzner, Israel M. *The Meaning of the Market Process.* New York: Routledge, 2002.

Storr, Virgil Henry. *Understanding the Culture of Markets*. New York: Routledge, 2013.

Von Mises, Ludwig. *Human Action: A Treatise on Economics*. Indianapolis: Liberty Fund, 2007. First published 1949 by Yale University Press.

Institutions and Culture

Alchian, Armen A. "Uncertainty, Evolution, and Economic Theory." *The Journal of Political Economy* 58, no. 3 (1950): 211–21.

Aligica, Paul Dragos, and Peter J. Boettke. *Challenging Institutional Analysis and Development: The Bloomington School*. New York: Routledge, 2009.

Coase, Ronald H. *The Firm, The Market, and the Law*. Chicago: University of Chicago Press, 1990.

Coyne, Christopher J. *Doing Bad by Doing Good: Why Humanitarian Action Fails*. Stanford, CA: Stanford University Press, 2013.

McCloskey, Deirdre N. *Bourgeois Dignity: Why Economics Can't Explain the Modern World*. Chicago: University of Chicago Press, 2011.

North, Douglass C. *Institutions, Institutional Change and Economic Performance*. Cambridge: Cambridge University Press, 1990.

Ostrom, Elinor C. *Governing the Commons: The Evolution of Institutions for Collective Action*. Cambridge: Cambridge University Press, 1990.

The Political Process

Buchanan, James M. *The Limits of Liberty: Between Anarchy and Leviathan*. Vol. 7 of *The Collected Works of James M. Buchanan*. Indianapolis: Liberty Fund, 2000. First published 1975 by University of Chicago Press.

Buchanan, James M., and Gordon Tullock. *The Calculus of Consent: Logical Foundations of Constitutional Democracy*. Vol. 3 of *The Collected Works of James M. Buchanan*. Indianapolis: Liberty Fund, 1999. First published 1962 by University of Michigan Press.

Higgs, Robert. *Crisis and Leviathan: Critical Episodes in the Growth of American Government*. 1987. 25th anniversary ed. Oakland, CA: Independent Institute, 2012.

Olson, Mancur. *The Logic of Collective Action: Public Goods and the Theory of Groups*. 1965. Second printing with new preface and appendix. Cambridge, MA: Harvard University Press, 1971.

Ostrom, Vincent. *The Meaning of Democracy and the Vulnerability of Democracies: A Response to Tocqueville's Challenge*. Ann Arbor, MI: University of Michigan Press, 1997.

Tullock, Gordon. *Virginia Political Economy*. Vol. 1 of *The Selected Works of Gordon Tullock*. Indianapolis: Liberty Fund, 2004.

Wagner, Richard E. *Politics as a Peculiar Business: Insights from a Theory of Entangled Political Economy*. Northampton, MA: Edward Elgar, 2016.

NOTES

1. An Enduring Puzzle

1. Adam Smith, *An Inquiry into the Nature and Causes of the Wealth of Nations* (1776; Indianapolis: Liberty Fund, 1981), book I, chapter 8.
2. Peter J. Boettke, *Living Economics: Yesterday, Today, and Tomorrow* (Oakland, CA: Independent Institute, 2012), xvi–xvii.
3. Ibid., xvii.
4. World Bank, "World Development Indicators," accessed September 15, 2016.
5. Angus Maddison, *The World Economy: A Millennial Perspective* (Paris: OECD, 2006), 30.
6. United Nations Population Fund, "International Migration 2013," accessed July 28, 2015.
7. Sakiko Fukada-Parr et al., *Human Development Report 2004: Cultural Liberty in Today's Diverse World* (New York: United Nations Development Programme, 2004).
8. Robert William Fogel, *The Escape from Hunger and Premature Death, 1700–2100: Europe, America, and the Third World* (Cambridge: Cambridge University Press, 2004).
9. Ibid.
10. In an influential 1974 study, Richard Easterlin found that within countries, higher income was associated with greater happiness. Paradoxically, he also found that across countries and across time, more income did not seem to be associated with greater happiness. Known as the "Easterlin paradox," this finding prompted many to conclude that, once people obtain a certain level of income, further absolute income gains do not lead to greater happiness. See Richard A. Easterlin, "Does Economic Growth Improve the Human Lot? Some Empirical Evidence," in *Nations and Households in Economic Growth: Essays in Honor of Moses Abramovitz*, ed. P. A. David and Melvin W. Reder (New York: Academic Press, 1974). Newer studies, however, challenge the original Easterlin finding. Using a larger dataset with more years and more countries, Betsey Stevenson and Justin Wolfers found that higher income across countries and across time was, indeed, associated with higher

levels of subjective well-being. See Betsey Stevenson and Justin Wolfers, "Economic Growth and Subjective Well-Being: Reassessing the Easterlin Paradox," *Brookings Papers on Economic Activity* 39, no. 1 (Spring 2008): 1–102. Similar results have been obtained by Ruut Veenhoven, "Is Happiness Relative?," *Social Indicators Research* 24, no. 1 (February 1991): 1–34; Ronald Inglehart and Hans-Dieter Klingemann, "Genes, Culture, Democracy, and Happiness," in *Culture and Subjective Well-Being*, ed. Edward Diener and Eunkook M. Suh (Cambridge, MA: Bradford Books, 2003); Michael R. Hagerty and Ruut Veenhoven, "Wealth and Happiness Revisited: Growing Wealth of Nations *Does* Go with Greater Happiness," *Social Indicators Research* 64 (2003): 1–27; Ed Diener, Marissa Diener, and Carol Diener, "Factors Predicting the Subjective Well-Being of Nations," in *Culture and Well-Being*, ed. Ed Diener (Dordrecht, Netherlands: Springer 2009), 43–70. The newer results do seem to indicate that when national income rises, the short-term boost in happiness is greater than the long-term boost (see, especially, Hagerty and Veenhoven, "Wealth and Happiness Revisited"). Apparently, as time passes, people tend to adjust to their new, higher level of income, and their view of what constitutes prosperity adjusts upward. See Ronald Inglehart, *Culture Shift in Advanced Industrial Society* (Princeton, NJ: Princeton University Press, 1990).

11. Bruce Yandle, Maya Vijayaraghavan, and Madhusudan Bhattarai, "The Environmental Kuznets Curve: A Primer" (PERC Research Study, Property and Environmental Research Center, Bozeman, MT, May 2002).

12. This phenomenon is known as the "Flynn effect." See Ian J. Deary, *Intelligence: A Very Short Introduction* (Oxford: Oxford University Press, 2001).

13. Benjamin M. Friedman, *The Moral Consequences of Economic Growth* (New York: Vintage, 2006), 4.

14. Suzy Khimm, "Does America's 99 Percent Represent the Top 1 Percent on Earth?" *Washington Post*, October 12, 2011. There are many countries in which prosperity is not widely shared. Brazil, for example, has some of the world's highest and lowest income earners. For more details, see Branko Milanovic, *The Haves and the Have-Nots: A Brief and Idiosyncratic History of Global Inequality* (New York: Basic Books, 2012).

15. Alberto F. Ades and Edward L. Glaeser, "Evidence on Growth, Increasing Returns, and the Extent of the Market," *Quarterly Journal of Economics* 114, no. 3 (1999): 1025–45.

16. Robert M. Solow, "A Contribution to the Theory of Economic Growth," *Quarterly Journal of Economics* 70, no. 1 (February 1956): 65–94.

17. David E. Bloom and Jeffrey D. Sachs, "Geography, Demography, and Economic Growth in Africa," *Brookings Papers on Economic Activity* 29, no. 2 (1998): 207–96; Jeffrey D. Sachs and Andrew M. Warner, "Natural Resource Abundance and Economic Growth" (NBER Working Paper No. 5398, National Bureau of Economic Research, December 1995); John Luke Gallup and Jeffrey D. Sachs, "The Economic Burden of Malaria," *American Journal of Tropical Medicine and Hygiene* 64, no. 1–2, suppl (February 2001): 85–96; Jeffrey D. Sachs, "Institutions Don't Rule: Direct Effects of Geography on Per Capita Income" (NBER Working Paper No. 9490, National Bureau of Economic Research, February 2003).

18. Jared Diamond, *Guns, Germs, and Steel: The Fates of Human Societies* (New York: W. W. Norton, 1999).

19. Gregory Clark, *A Farewell to Alms: A Brief Economic History of the World* (Princeton, NJ: Princeton University Press, 2009).

20. David S. Landes, *The Wealth and Poverty of Nations: Why Some Are So Rich and Some So Poor* (New York: W. W. Norton, 1999).

21. Daron Acemoglu and James Robinson, *Why Nations Fail: The Origins of Power, Prosperity, and Poverty* (New York: Crown Business, 2012).

22. Joel Mokyr, *The Gifts of Athena: Historical Origins of the Knowledge Economy* (Princeton, NJ: Princeton University Press, 2005).

23. Deirdre N. McCloskey, "How the West (and the Rest) Got Rich," *Wall Street Journal*, May 20, 2016.

24. Deirdre N. McCloskey, *Bourgeois Dignity: Why Economics Can't Explain the Modern World* (Chicago: University of Chicago Press, 2010).

25. The most common technique is ordinary least squares (OLS), which achieves this estimate by finding the best fit of a line through a scatter plot of data. In this case, the

best-fitting line is that which minimizes the sum of the squared differences between the line and the observed dependent variable.

26. Peter Kennedy offers the following five assumptions of the classical linear regression model: (1) "The dependent variable can be calculated as a linear function of a specific set of independent variables, plus a disturbance term"; (2) "The expected value of the disturbance term is zero"; (3) "The disturbance terms all have the same variance and are not correlated with one another"; (4) "The observations on the independent variable can be considered fixed in repeated samples"; and (5) "The number of observations is greater than the number of independent variables and that there are no exact linear relationships between the independent variables." Peter E. Kennedy, *A Guide to Econometrics*, 5th ed. (Cambridge, MA: MIT Press, 2003), 48–49.

27. More precisely, this problem occurs in a multi-equation system, such as supply and demand, in which equations have variables in common, such as price and quantity. Observations on quantity and price alone will not allow one to trace out (identify) either the supply curve or the demand curve because it is impossible to determine which curve or curves have moved. It *is* possible, however, to identify the supply and demand curves if one finds other variables that are associated with the movement of only one curve or the other. Franklin M. Fisher, *The Identification Problem in Econometrics*, illus. ed. (Huntington, NY: Krieger, 1966).

28. Tyler Cowen and Alexander T. Tabarrok, *Modern Principles of Economics* (New York: Worth Publishers, 2009), 40.

29. Vernon L. Smith, "An Experimental Study of Competitive Market Behavior," *Journal of Political Economy* 70, no. 2 (April 1962): 111–37.

30. Elinor Ostrom, "A Behavioral Approach to the Rational Choice Theory of Collective Action: Presidential Address, American Political Science Association, 1997," *American Political Science Review* 92, no. 1 (March 1998): 1–22.

31. Vernon L. Smith, Gerry L. Suchanek, and Arlington W. Williams, "Bubbles, Crashes, and Endogenous Expectations in Experimental Spot Asset Markets," *Econometrica* 56, no. 5 (1988): 1119–51.

32. For an important critique, see Edward E. Leamer, "Let's Take the Con Out of Econometrics," *American Economic Review* 73, no. 1 (1983): 31–43.

33. Joshua D. Angrist and Alan B. Krueger, "Empirical Strategies in Labor Economics," in *Handbook of Labor Economics*, ed. Orley Ashenfelter and David Card, vol. 3, part A (Amsterdam: Elsevier, 1999), 1277–366.

34. Steven D. Levitt, "Using Electoral Cycles in Police Hiring to Estimate the Effect of Police on Crime," *American Economic Review* 87, no. 3 (June 1997): 270–90. Levitt has become famous (for an economist) for deploying clever instruments to test tricky questions. For more, see his bestseller, coauthored with Stephen Dubner. Steven D. Levitt and Stephen J. Dubner, *Freakonomics: A Rogue Economist Explores the Hidden Side of Everything* (New York: William Morrow, 2009), 1.

35. Joshua D. Angrist and Victor Lavy, "Using Maimonides' Rule to Estimate the Effect of Class Size on Scholastic Achievement," *Quarterly Journal of Economics* 114, no. 2 (1999): 533–75.

36. John J. Donohue and Justin Wolfers, "Uses and Abuses of Empirical Evidence in the Death Penalty Debate," *Stanford Law Review* 58, no. 3 (September 2005): 791.

37. These are known as "two-way fixed-effects regressions."

38. James H. Stock and Francesco Trebbi, "Retrospectives: Who Invented Instrumental Variable Regression?" *Journal of Economic Perspectives* 17, no. 3 (Summer 2003): 177–94.

39. Joshua D. Angrist and Jörn-Steffen Pischke, "The Credibility Revolution in Empirical Economics: How Better Research Design Is Taking the Con Out of Econometrics" (NBER Working Paper No. 15794, National Bureau of Economic Research, March 2010).

40. Tjalling C. Koopmans, "Measurement without Theory," *Review of Economics and Statistics* 29, no. 3 (August 1947): 161–72.

41. Russ Roberts, "James Heckman on Facts, Evidence, and the State of Econometrics," *EconTalk* podcast, Library of Economics and Liberty, January 25, 2016.

42. Milton Friedman, "The Fed's Thermostat," *Wall Street Journal*, August 19, 2003.

43. See condition 5 listed in note 26.

44. Isaac Ehrlich, "The Deterrent Effect of Capital Punishment: A Question of Life and Death," *American Economic Review* 65, no. 3 (June 1975): 397–417; Angrist and Pischke, "Credibility Revolution in Empirical Economics," 6.

45. Angrist and Pischke, "Credibility Revolution in Empirical Economics," 4.

46. James Heckman details a number of cases in which this was a problem. See Roberts, "James Heckman on Facts, Evidence, and the State of Econometrics."

47. See, again, note 26 above.

48. Robert E. Lucas Jr., "Econometric Policy Evaluation: A Critique," *Carnegie-Rochester Conference Series on Public Policy* 1, no. 1 (1976): 41.

49. Mark L. Mitchell and Janina M. Jolley, *Research Design Explained*, 8th ed. (Belmont, CA: Wadsworth Publishing, 2012), 54.

50. Leamer, "Let's Take the Con Out of Econometrics."

51. Jeffrey D. Sachs and Andrew M. Warner, "Economic Reform and the Process of Global Integration," *Brookings Papers on Economic Activity* 26, no. 1, 25th anniversary issue (1995).

52. Diamond, *Guns, Germs, and Steel*; Gallup and Sachs, "Economic Burden of Malaria."

53. "There are in Africa none of those great inlets, such as the Baltic and Adriatic seas in Europe, the Mediterranean and Euxine seas in both Europe and Asia, and the gulphs of Arabia, Persia, India, Bengal, and Siam, in Asia, to carry maritime commerce into the interior parts of that great continent: and the great rivers of Africa are at too great a distance from one another to give occasion to any considerable inland navigation." Smith, *Wealth of Nations*, book I, chapter 3.

54. Michael L. Ross, "The Political Economy of the Resource Curse," *World Politics* 51, no. 2 (January 1999): 297–322; William Easterly and Ross Levine, "Tropics, Germs, and Crops: How Endowments Influence Economic Development," *Journal of Monetary Economics* 50, no. 1 (January 2003): 3–39; Michael L. Ross, *The Oil Curse: How Petroleum Wealth Shapes the Development of Nations* (Princeton, NJ: Princeton University Press, 2013).

55. Dani Rodrik, "Institutions, Integration, and Geography: In Search of the Deep Determinants of Economic Growth" (Working Paper, Weatherhead Center for International Affairs, Harvard University, Cambridge, MA, February 2002).

56. Edward L. Glaeser et al., "Do Institutions Cause Growth?," *Journal of Economic Growth* 9, no. 3 (September 2004): 271–303.

57. Mark Duggan and Steven D. Levitt, "Winning Isn't Everything: Corruption in Sumo Wrestling," *American Economic Review* 92, no. 5 (December 2002): 1594–1605; Steven D. Levitt, "Testing Theories of Discrimination: Evidence from 'Weakest Link,'" *Journal of Law and Economics* 47, no. 2 (2004): 431–52.

58. Quoted in Noam Scheiber, "Freaks and Geeks; How Freakonomics Is Ruining the Dismal Science," *New Republic*, April 2, 2007.

59. Nadwa Mossaad, "U.S. Lawful Permanent Residents: 2014," Department of Homeland Security, April 2016.

60. To be precise, "a Mexican-born worker increases her or his wage 4.15 times just by crossing the United States–Mexico border." Those who migrate to the interior of the United States increase their wages 5.34 times. These numbers account for differences in purchasing power in the two countries. Ernesto Aguayo Téllez and Christian Rivera-Mendoza, "Migration from Mexico to the United States: Wage Benefits of Crossing the Border and Going to the U.S. Interior," *Politics & Policy* 39, no. 1 (2011): 132.

61. The gains from immigration could be much greater if they were not managed. Benjamin Powell, "The Economics of Immigration: An Austrian Contribution," *Review of Austrian Economics* 29, no. 4 (2016): 343–49.

62. "GDP per Capita (Current US$)," World Bank, 2015.

63. Kirk Hamilton et al., *Where Is the Wealth of Nations? Measuring Capital for the 21st Century* (Washington, DC: World Bank, 2006).

64. Economists figure that "intangible capital" accounts for about 77 percent of all capital. Ibid., 26.

65. McCloskey, *Bourgeois Dignity*.

66. Virgil Henry Storr, *Understanding the Culture of Markets* (New York: Routledge, 2013).

2. The Core Themes of Mainline Economics

1. Smith, *Wealth of Nations*, book I, chapter 2.

2. Justin Lahart, "Economist Scraps Hepatitis Theory on China's 'Missing Women,'" *Wall Street Journal*, May 22, 2008.

3. Paul Gertler, Manisha Shah, and Stefano M. Bertozzi, "Risky Business: The Market for Unprotected Commercial Sex," *Journal of Political Economy* 113, no. 3 (June 2005): 518–50.

4. Quoted in James M. Buchanan, "What Should Economists Do?," *Southern Economic Journal* 30, no. 3 (January 1964): 213–22.

5. The roots of mainline economics go back at least as far as Thomas Aquinas of the 13th century. Other contributors include 15th- and 16th-century Late Scholastics at the University of Salamanca in Spain; 18th-century Scottish Enlightenment thinkers—especially David Hume, Adam Smith, and Adam Ferguson; 19th-century French liberals Jean-Baptiste Say and Frédéric Bastiat; and 20th-century thinkers in the early neoclassical tradition, such as Carl Menger, Ludwig von Mises, and F. A. Hayek. Boettke, *Living Economics*, xvi.

6. Peter J. Boettke, "Liberty vs. Power in Economic Policy in the 20th and 21st Centuries," *Journal of Private Enterprise* 22, no. 2 (Spring 2007): 7; *Mainline Economics: Six Nobel Lectures in the Tradition of Adam Smith*, ed. Peter J. Boettke, Stefanie Haeffele-Balch, and Virgil Henry Storr (Arlington, VA: Mercatus Center at George Mason University, 2016).

7. F. A. Hayek, "The Intellectuals and Socialism," *University of Chicago Law Review* 16, no. 3 (Spring 1949): 432.

8. Smith, *Wealth of Nations*, book I, chapter 2.

9. This is why, when Hayek moved his research interests from the narrow technical economics of imputation theory to the broader social philosophical projects of *The Road to Serfdom* and *The Constitution of Liberty*, he was not abandoning economics per se but trying to encourage his fellow economists to pay attention to the institutional framework within which economic life is played out.

10. James M. Buchanan, "The Domain of Constitutional Economics," *Constitutional Political Economy* 1, no. 1 (December 1990): 13.

11. James M. Buchanan, *Cost and Choice: An Inquiry in Economic Theory* (Indianapolis: Liberty Fund, 1969).

12. Sam Peltzman, "The Effects of Automobile Safety Regulation," *Journal of Political Economy* 83, no. 4 (1975): 677–725.

13. Cowen and Tabarrok, *Modern Principles of Economics*, 1.
14. Israel M. Kirzner, "Hayek, the Nobel, and the Revival of Austrian Economics," *Review of Austrian Economics* 28, no. 3 (September 2015): 225–36.
15. Smith, *Wealth of Nations*, book I, chapter 2.
16. Ronald H. Coase, "The Federal Communications Commission," *Journal of Law and Economics* 2 (October 1959): 18.
17. See John Locke, *Two Treatises of Government*, ed. Mark Goldie (1689; London: J. M. Dent, 1993); David Hume, *A Treatise of Human Nature* (1739; Oxford: Clarendon Press, 1896); Robert Nozick, *Anarchy, State, and Utopia* (New York: Basic Books, 1974); David Schmidtz, *The Elements of Justice* (Cambridge: Cambridge University Press, 2006).
18. Armen A. Alchian, "Property Rights," in *The Concise Encyclopedia of Economics*, ed. David Henderson (Indianapolis: Liberty Fund, 2008).
19. Randy T. Simmons, *Beyond Politics: The Roots of Government Failure* (Oakland, CA: Independent Institute, 2011), 131.
20. Alchian, "Property Rights."
21. Ibid.
22. Garrett Hardin, "The Tragedy of the Commons," *Science* 162, no. 3859 (December 1968): 1243–48.
23. Tyler Cowen, "Public Goods and Externalities," in *The Concise Encyclopedia of Economics*, ed. David Henderson (Indianapolis: Liberty Fund, 1993).
24. Richard E. Wagner, *Deficits, Debt, and Democracy: Wrestling with Tragedy on the Fiscal Commons* (Cheltenham, UK: Edward Elgar, 2012).
25. Ludwig von Mises, *Economic Calculation in the Socialist Commonwealth* (1920; Auburn, AL: Ludwig von Mises Institute, 1990). For a comprehensive account of the socialist calculation debate, see Peter Boettke, ed., *Socialism and the Market: The Socialist Calculation Debate Revisited* (London: Routledge, 2000).
26. Lawrence W. Reed, "Mises and the Soviet Free Market," in *The Free Market Reader*, ed. Llewellyn H. Rockwell Jr. (Auburn, AL: Ludwig von Mises Institute, 1988), 237.
27. Douglass C. North and Barry R. Weingast, "Constitutions and Commitment: The Evolution of Institutions Governing Public Choice in Seventeenth-Century England," *Journal of*

Economic History 49, no. 4 (December 1989): 803–32. For a dissenting view, see McCloskey, *Bourgeois Dignity*.

28. J. Bradford De Long and Andrei Shleifer, "Princes and Merchants: European City Growth before the Industrial Revolution," *Journal of Law and Economics* 36, no. 2 (October 1993): 671–702; Stephen Knack and Philip Keefer, "Institutions and Economic Performance: Cross-Country Tests Using Alternative Institutional Measures," *Economics & Politics* 7, no. 3 (November 1995): 207–27; Robert E. Hall and Charles I. Jones, "Why Do Some Countries Produce So Much More Output per Worker Than Others?" *Quarterly Journal of Economics* 114, no. 1 (February 1999): 83–116; Daron Acemoglu, Simon Johnson, and James A. Robinson, "The Colonial Origins of Comparative Development: An Empirical Investigation," *American Economic Review* 91, no. 5 (December 2001): 1369–401; Dani Rodrik, Arvind Subramanian, and Francesco Trebbi, "Institutions Rule: The Primacy of Institutions over Geography and Integration in Economic Development," *Journal of Economic Growth* 9, no. 2 (June 2004): 131–65.

29. F. A. Hayek, "The Pretense of Knowledge," *American Economic Review* 79, no. 6 (December 1989): 3, quoted in *Mainline Economics*, ed. Boettke, Haeffele-Balch, and Storr, 25.

30. Tyler Cowen, *The Great Stagnation: How America Ate All the Low-Hanging Fruit of Modern History, Got Sick, and Will (Eventually) Feel Better* (New York, NY: Dutton, 2011).

31. Ryan Decker et al., "The Role of Entrepreneurship in US Job Creation and Economic Dynamism," *Journal of Economic Perspectives* 28, no. 3 (2014): 3–24.

32. Donald J. Boudreaux et al., *What America's Decline in Economic Freedom Means for Entrepreneurship and Prosperity* (Arlington, VA: Mercatus Center at George Mason University, 2015); Liya Palagashvili, "Strive to Help Entrepreneurs Thrive," *U.S. News & World Report*, April 15, 2015.

33. Laurence Kotlikoff, "Assessing Fiscal Sustainability" (Mercatus Research, Mercatus Center at George Mason University, Arlington, VA, December 12, 2013).

34. Hester Peirce and James Broughel, *Dodd-Frank: What It Does and Why It's Flawed* (Arlington, VA: Mercatus Center at George Mason University, 2013), 63.

35. David Hume, *Essays: Moral, Political, and Literary*, rev. ed. (Indianapolis: Liberty Fund, 1985), 42.

36. Hayek, "Pretense of Knowledge," 7, quoted in *Mainline Economics*, ed. Boettke, Haeffele-Balch, and Storr, 38.

3. Market Process Economics

1. Elements of this chapter are adapted from Peter J. Boettke, "Austrian School of Economics," in *The Concise Encyclopedia of Economics*, ed. David Henderson (Indianapolis: Liberty Fund, 2008); Peter J. Boettke, "Introduction," in *Handbook on Contemporary Austrian Economics* (Cheltenham, UK: Edward Elgar, 2012).
2. F. A. Hayek, "Pretense of Knowledge," 7, quoted in *Mainline Economics*, ed. Boettke, Haeffele-Balch, and Storr, 38.
3. Smith, *Wealth of Nations*, book I, chapter 2.
4. Matt Ridley, *The Rational Optimist: How Prosperity Evolves*, reprint ed. (New York: Harper Perennial, 2011), 56. Ridley notes an exception for one type of exchange: many species other than humans trade food for sex.
5. F. A. Hayek, *Law, Legislation and Liberty, Volume 2: The Mirage of Social Justice* (Chicago: University of Chicago Press, 1978), 108.
6. Note that the Mercatus Center was once called the Center for the Study of Market Processes.
7. Virgil Henry Storr, "The Facts of the Social Sciences Are What People Believe and Think," in *Handbook on Contemporary Austrian Economics*, ed. Peter J. Boettke (Cheltenham, UK: Edward Elgar, 2010), 67–76.
8. Buchanan, *Cost and Choice*.
9. The French economist Frédéric Bastiat first developed the concept of opportunity cost. Frédéric Bastiat, "What Is Seen and What Is Not Seen," in *Selected Essays on Political Economy*, trans. Seymour Cain (1848; Irvington-on-Hudson, NY: Foundation for Economic Education, 1995.)
10. F. A. Hayek, "The Use of Knowledge in Society," *American Economic Review* 35, no. 4 (September 1945): 521.
11. Ibid., 526.
12. Paul W. MacAvoy, "The Regulation-Induced Shortage of Natural Gas," *Journal of Law and Economics* 14, no. 1 (1971): 167–99.
13. Frank H. Knight, "Immutable Law in Economics: Its Reality and Limitations," *American Economic Review* 36, no. 2 (May 1946): 102.

14. Joseph A. Schumpeter, *Capitalism, Socialism and Democracy* (New York: Harper & Brothers), 132.
15. Joseph A. Schumpeter, *The Theory of Economic Development: An Inquiry into Profits, Capital, Credit, Interest, and the Business Cycle*, ed. John E. Elliott (New Brunswick, NJ: Transaction Publishers, 1912), 66.
16. Israel M. Kirzner, *Competition and Entrepreneurship* (Chicago: University of Chicago Press, 1973), 15–16.
17. Entrepreneurship can be characterized by three distinct moments: serendipity (discovery), search (conscious deliberation), and seizing the opportunity for profit.
18. George A. Akerlof, "The Market for 'Lemons': Quality Uncertainty and the Market Mechanism," *Quarterly Journal of Economics* 84, no. 3 (August 1970): 488–500.
19. Adam Thierer et al., "How the Internet, the Sharing Economy and Reputational Feedback Mechanisms Solve the 'Lemons Problem'" (Mercatus Working Paper, Mercatus Center at George Mason University, Arlington, VA, June 2015). On reputation mechanisms in e-commerce, see Mark Steckbeck and Peter J. Boettke, "Turning Lemons into Lemonade: Entrepreneurial Solutions in Adverse Selection Problems in E-Commerce," in *Markets, Information, and Communication: Austrian Perspectives on the Internet Economy*, ed. Jack Birner and Pierre Garrouste (New York: Routledge, 2004). On the market for reputation, see F. A. Hayek, "The Meaning of Competition," in *Individualism and Economic Order*, reissue ed. (Chicago: University of Chicago Press, 1996).
20. F. A. Hayek, "Competition as a Discovery Procedure," trans. Marcellus S. Snow, *Quarterly Journal of Austrian Economics* 5, no. 3 (Fall 2002): 9–23.
21. Adam Ferguson, *An Essay on the History of Civil Society*, 5th ed. (London: T. Cadell, 1782), 205.
22. Thomas C. Schelling, "Models of Segregation," *American Economic Review* 59, no. 2 (May 1969): 488–93. For more examples of both good and bad spontaneous orders, see Nozick, *Anarchy, State, and Utopia*, 20–21. And for a discussion of perverse spontaneous orders, see Nona P. Martin and Virgil Henry Storr, "On Perverse Emergent Orders," *Studies in Emergent Order* 1 (2008): 73–91.
23. F. A. Hayek, *Prices and Production*, 2nd ed. (London: Routledge, 1932); F. A. Hayek, "Armen A. Alchian Interviews

Friedrich A. Hayek (Part I)," *The Hayek Interviews: Alive and Influential*, video series, November 11, 1978; Peter J. Boettke, *Calculation and Coordination: Essays on Socialism and Transitional Political Economy* (London: Routledge, 2001).

24. John Adams, *Novanglus, Thoughts on Government, Defence of the Constitution*, vol. 4 of *The Works of John Adams, Second President of the United States: With a Life of the Author, Notes and Illustrations, by His Grandson Charles Francis Adams* (Boston, MA: Little, Brown, 1856), 404.

25. F. A. Hayek, *The Road to Serfdom: Text and Documents—The Definitive Edition*, ed. Bruce Caldwell (Chicago: University of Chicago Press, 1944), 112.

26. The central bank may be able to boost growth and reduce the unemployment rate if it can fool businesses into thinking that the increased prices that their customers are willing to pay are not a generalized inflation. This only works, however, so long as the public can be fooled. Once the public catches on, the central bank must resort to ever-larger rates of inflation in order to surprise the public. Robert E. Lucas Jr., "Expectations and the Neutrality of Money," *Journal of Economic Theory* 4, no. 2 (April 1972): 103–24; Lucas Jr., "Econometric Policy Evaluation."

27. Walter Bagehot, *Lombard Street: A Description of the Money Market* (1873; Lexington, KY: CreateSpace Independent Publishing Platform, 2013), 78.

28. Finn E. Kydland and Edward C. Prescott, "Rules Rather Than Discretion: The Inconsistency of Optimal Plans," *Journal of Political Economy* 85, no. 3 (1977): 473–91.

29. John Taylor, "Discretion versus Policy Rules in Practice," *Carnegie-Rochester Conference Series on Public Policy* 39, no. 1 (1993): 195–214; Milton Friedman, *The Optimum Quantity of Money*, rev. ed., ed. Michael D. Bordo (1969; New Brunswick, NJ: Aldine Transaction, 1969); F. A. Hayek, *Full Employment at Any Price?* (London: Transatlantic Arts, 1975). For a reconstruction of Hayek's views, see Lawrence H. White, "Hayek's Monetary Theory and Policy: A Critical Reconstruction," *Journal of Money, Credit and Banking* 31, no. 1 (1999): 109–20; Scott Sumner, "The Case for Nominal GDP Targeting" (Mercatus Research, Mercatus Center at George Mason University, Arlington, VA, October 23, 2012).

30. The widely lauded goal of a politically independent central bank is one aspect of the rules-based approach to monetary policy.

Despite the wide acceptance of this rule, there is much evidence to suggest that central banks are far from independent of political influence. Richard E. Wagner, "Boom and Bust: The Political Economy of Economic Disorder," in *The Theory of Public Choice, II,* ed. James M. Buchanan and Robert D. Tollison (Ann Arbor: University of Michigan Press, 1984), 238–72; Burton A. Abrams, "How Richard Nixon Pressured Arthur Burns: Evidence from the Nixon Tapes," *Journal of Economic Perspectives* 20, no. 4 (2006): 177–88; Daniel J. Smith and Peter J. Boettke, "An Episodic History of Modern Fed Independence," *Independent Review* 20, no. 1 (Summer 2015): 99–120.

31. Lawrence H. White, "The Federal Reserve and the Rule of Law" (Testimony before the Subcommittee on Monetary Policy and Trade, House Committee on Financial Services, Mercatus Center at George Mason University, Arlington, VA, September 11, 2013), 6.

32. For two examples, see Buchanan and Wagner on a balanced budget rule and Randy Barnett on constitutional rules cabining regulatory powers. James M. Buchanan and Richard E. Wagner, *Democracy in Deficit: The Political Legacy of Lord Keynes* (Indianapolis: Liberty Fund, 1977); Randy E. Barnett, *Restoring the Lost Constitution: The Presumption of Liberty* (Princeton, NJ: Princeton University Press, 2013).

33. George Selgin and Lawrence H. White, "A Fiscal Theory of Government's Role in Money," *Economic Inquiry* 37, no. 1 (January 1999): 154–65; Peter J. Boettke and Christopher J. Coyne, "The Debt-Inflation Cycle and the Global Financial Crisis," *Global Policy* 2, no. 2 (May 2011): 184–89.

34. Hayek, "Competition as a Discovery Procedure."

35. Kirzner, "Hayek, the Nobel, and the Revival of Austrian Economics."

36. Jerry Ellig, "Railroad Deregulation and Consumer Welfare," *Journal of Regulatory Economics* 21, no. 2 (2002): 143–67.

37. Adam Thierer, *Permissionless Innovation: The Continuing Case for Comprehensive Technological Freedom* (Arlington, VA: Mercatus Center at George Mason University, 2014).

38. Christopher Koopman, Matthew Mitchell, and Adam Thierer, "The Sharing Economy and Consumer Protection Regulation: The Case for Policy Change," *Journal of Business, Entrepreneurship & the Law* 8, no. 2 (2015): 530–45; Matthew D.

Mitchell and Michael Farren, "If You Like Uber, You Would've Loved the Jitney," *Los Angeles Times*, July 12, 2014; Matthew D. Mitchell, "Share and Share Alike," *U.S. News & World Report*, April 15, 2014; Matthew D. Mitchell, "Transportation Apps Offer Alternative to Taxis," *Richmond Times-Dispatch*, June 14, 2014.

39. Christopher Koopman, Matthew D. Mitchell, and Adam Thierer, Public Interest Comment for Federal Trade Commission Workshop, "The 'Sharing' Economy: Issues Facing Platforms, Participants, and Regulators" (Public Interest Comment, Mercatus Center at George Mason University, Arlington, VA, June 2015).

40. Emily Chamlee-Wright and Virgil Henry Storr, "The Role of Social Entrepreneurship in Post-Katrina Community Recovery," in *The Political Economy of Hurricane Katrina and Community Rebound*, ed. Emily Chamlee-Wright and Virgil Henry Storr (Cheltenham, UK: Edward Elgar, 2010).

41. Virgil Henry Storr, Stefanie Haeffele-Balch, and Laura E. Grube, *Community Revival in the Wake of Disaster: Lessons in Local Entrepreneurship* (New York: Palgrave Macmillan, 2015).

42. Steven Horwitz, "Making Hurricane Response More Effective: Lessons from the Private Sector and the Coast Guard during Katrina," in *The Political Economy of Hurricane Katrina and Community Rebound*, ed. Emily Chamlee-Wright and Virgil Henry Storr (Cheltenham, UK: Edward Elgar, 2010).

43. Ibid., 49.

44. Gerald F. Seib, "In Crisis, Opportunity for Obama," *Wall Street Journal*, November 21, 2008.

45. For a particularly insightful treatment of this subject, see Robert Higgs, *Crisis and Leviathan: Critical Episodes in the Growth of American Government*, 25th anniversary ed. (1987; Oakland, CA: Independent Institute, 2013).

46. Milton Friedman, *Capitalism and Freedom*, 40th anniversary ed. (Chicago: University of Chicago Press, 2002), xiv.

47. Russ Roberts, "Gambling with Other People's Money," *Cafe Hayek*, April 28, 2010.

48. Gretchen Morgenson, *Reckless Endangerment: How Outsized Ambition, Greed, and Corruption Led to Economic Armageddon* (New York: Times Books, 2011), 16.

49. Matthew D. Mitchell, *The Pathology of Privilege: The Economic Consequences of Government Favoritism* (Arlington, VA: Mercatus Center at George Mason University, 2014), 14.

50. Arnold Kling, *Not What They Had in Mind: A History of Policies That Produced the Financial Crisis of 2008* (Arlington, VA: Mercatus Center at George Mason University, 2009).

51. Lawrence J. White, "An Assessment of the Credit Rating Agencies: Background, Analysis, and Policy" (Mercatus Working Paper, Mercatus Center at George Mason University, Arlington, VA, September 10, 2013).

52. Steven Horwitz and Peter J. Boettke, *The House That Uncle Sam Built: The Untold Story of the Great Recession of 2008* (Irvington-on-Hudson, NY: Foundation for Economic Education, 2009).

53. Casey B. Mulligan, *The Redistribution Recession: How Labor Market Distortions Contracted the Economy* (New York: Oxford University Press, 2012).

54. Ibid., 132.

55. Casey B. Mulligan, "The Affordable Care Act and the New Economics of Part-Time Work" (Mercatus Working Paper, Mercatus Center at George Mason University, Arlington, VA, October 2014).

4. Institutions and Culture

1. Ronald H. Coase, "The Institutional Structure of Production," *American Economic Review* 82, no. 4 (September 1992): 716, quoted in *Mainline Economics*, ed. Boettke, Haeffele-Balch, and Storr, 70.

2. Douglass C. North, *Institutions, Institutional Change and Economic Performance* (Cambridge: Cambridge University Press, 1990), 3.

3. The "new" in "new institutional economics" distinguishes the school from "old" or "traditional" institutional economics, which is far more critical of neoclassical economics.

4. Carl J. Dahlman, "The Problem of Externality," *Journal of Law and Economics* 22, no. 1 (1979): 147–48.

5. Ronald H. Coase, "The Nature of the Firm," *Economica* 4, no. 16 (1937): 390.

6. Coase, "Federal Communications Commission"; Ronald H. Coase, "The Problem of Social Cost," *Journal of Law and Economics* 3 (October 1960): 1–44.

7. Karen Grigsby Bates, "Condiment Detente: Sriracha Plant to Stay in California City," NPR, May 29, 2015.

8. A. C. Pigou, *The Economics of Welfare*, reprint ed. (London: Macmillan, 1920).

9. John V. Nye, "The Pigou Problem," *Regulation* 31, no. 2 (Summer 2008).

10. Coase, "Problem of Social Cost," 2.

11. Ibid.

12. Coase, "Federal Communications Commission," 27.

13. George J. Stigler, *The Theory of Price*, 3rd ed. (New York: Macmillan, 1966), 113.

14. Ronald H. Coase, *The Firm, the Market, and the Law* (Chicago: University of Chicago Press, 1974), 174.

15. Oliver E. Williamson, "Transaction-Cost Economics: The Governance of Contractual Relations," *Journal of Law and Economics* 22, no. 2 (October 1979): 233.

16. Douglass C. North, "Economic Performance through Time," *American Economic Review* 84, no. 3 (June 1994): 361, quoted in *Mainline Economics*, ed. Boettke, Haeffele-Balch, and Storr, 86.

17. Rodrik, Subramanian, and Trebbi, "Institutions Rule."

18. Stanley L. Engerman and Kenneth L. Sokoloff, "Factor Endowments, Inequality, and Paths of Development among New World Economics" (NBER Working Paper No. 9259, National Bureau of Economic Research, October 2002); Acemoglu, Johnson, and Robinson, "Colonial Origins of Comparative Development"; Acemoglu and Robinson, *Why Nations Fail.*

19. Claudia R. Williamson, "Informal Institutions Rule: Institutional Arrangements and Economic Performance," *Public Choice* 139, no. 3–4 (June 2009): 371–87.

20. Peter J. Boettke, Christopher J. Coyne, and Peter T. Leeson, "Institutional Stickiness and the New Development Economics," *American Journal of Economics and Sociology* 67, no. 2 (April 2008): 331–58. Williamson extends their analysis and offers empirical evidence in support of it. Williamson, "Informal Institutions Rule." See also Svetozar Pejovich for a discussion of the role that informal rules play in the transition to a market economy. Svetozar Pejovich, "Understanding the Transaction Costs of Transition: It's the Culture, Stupid," *Review of Austrian Economics* 16, no. 4 (2003): 347–61.

21. Virgil Henry Storr, "The Market as a Social Space: On the Meaningful Extraeconomic Conversations That Can Occur

in Markets," *Review of Austrian Economics* 21, no. 2–3 (January 7, 2008): 148.

22. Storr, "Market as a Social Space."

23. Virgil Henry Storr, *Understanding the Culture of Markets* (New York: Routledge, 2013), 4.

24. Smith, *Wealth of Nations*, book I, chapter 3 ("That the Division of Labour Is Limited by the Extent of the Market").

25. Quoted in Tim Harford, "The Economics of Trust," *Forbes*, November 3, 2006.

26. Peter T. Leeson, *Anarchy Unbound: Why Self-Governance Works Better Than You Think* (New York: Cambridge University Press, 2014).

27. Omar Al-Ubaydli et al., "The Causal Effect of Market Priming on Trust: An Experimental Investigation Using Randomized Control," *PLoS ONE* 8, no. 3 (March 5, 2013): e55968.

28. Matthew D. Mitchell, "Trust Me on This," *Neighborhood Effects*, Mercatus Center at George Mason University, Arlington, VA, October 24, 2011.

29. McCloskey, *Bourgeois Dignity*.

30. William J. Baumol, "Entrepreneurship: Productive, Unproductive, and Destructive," *Journal of Political Economy* 98, no. 5 (October 1990): 893–921. In a related paper, Murphy et al. show that per capita GDP growth is slower in those countries where a larger share of the population is engaged in unproductive entrepreneurship. Kevin M. Murphy, Andrei Shleifer, and Robert W. Vishny, "The Allocation of Talent: Implications for Growth," *Quarterly Journal of Economics* 106, no. 2 (May 1991): 503–30.

31. Alchian, "Property Rights."

32. James Gwartney, Robert A. Lawson, and Joshua Hall, *Economic Freedom of the World, 2013 Annual Report* (Vancouver, Canada: Fraser Institute, 2013).

33. Ibid.; William Ruger and Jason Sorens, *Freedom in the 50 States: An Index of Personal and Economic Freedom, 2013 Edition* (Mercatus Center at George Mason University, Arlington, VA, 2013).

34. Chris Doucouliagos and Mehmet Ali Ulubasoglu, "Economic Freedom and Economic Growth: Does Specification Make a Difference?," *European Journal of Political Economy* 22, no. 1 (March 2006): 60–81.

35. Joshua C. Hall and Robert A. Lawson, "Economic Freedom of the World: An Accounting of the Literature," *Contemporary Economic Policy* 32, no. 1 (2014): 1–19.

36. In other words, efficient policy is not always equilibrium policy, though critics sometimes confuse the two ideas. See, for example, Michael Lind, "The Question Libertarians Just Can't Answer," *Salon*, June 4, 2013. For a reply, see Matthew D. Mitchell, "Why Are There No Libertarian Countries?," *Neighborhood Effects*, Mercatus Center at George Mason University, Arlington, VA, June 17, 2013.

37. Thomas Jefferson, *The Works of Thomas Jefferson, Vol. 5 (Correspondence 1786–1789)*, federal ed., ed. Paul Leicester Ford (New York: G. P. Putnam's Sons, 1904).

38. James Madison, "The Bank Bill, House of Representatives," February 2, 1791, in *The Founders' Constitution*, Volume 3, Article 1, Section 8, Clause 18, Document 9 (Chicago: University of Chicago Press, 1987).

39. Kenneth A. Shepsle and Barry R. Weingast, "Structure-Induced Equilibrium and Legislative Choice," *Public Choice* 37, no. 3 (January 1981): 503–19.

40. Buchanan, "Domain of Constitutional Economics," 3. Emphasis original.

41. Buchanan and Wagner, *Democracy in Deficit*.

42. While Buchanan was comfortable theorizing about the optimal design of constitutional rules, Hayek was more skeptical, preferring rules that emerged over time to those that were "laid on."

43. Elinor Ostrom, "Beyond Markets and States: Polycentric Governance of Complex Economic Systems," *American Economic Review* 100, no. 3 (June 2010): 648, quoted in *Mainline Economics*, ed. Boettke, Haeffele-Balch, and Storr, 206.

44. F. A. Hayek, *The Constitution of Liberty* (Chicago: University of Chicago Press, 1960).

45. James M. Buchanan and Gordon Tullock, *The Calculus of Consent: Logical Foundations of Constitutional Democracy* (Ann Arbor: University of Michigan Press, 1962), chapter 16.

46. Michael Polanyi, *The Logic of Liberty* (1951; Indianapolis: Liberty Fund, 1998), 140n1.

47. For a thorough and state-of-the-art treatment of social norms, see Cristina Bicchieri, *The Grammar of Society: The Nature and Dynamics of Social Norms* (Cambridge: Cambridge

University Press, 2006); Robert Ellickson, *Order without Law: How Neighbors Settle Disputes* (Cambridge, MA: Harvard University Press, 1994).

48. Vincent Ostrom quoted in Paul Dragos Aligica and Peter J. Boettke, *Challenging Institutional Analysis and Development: The Bloomington School* (New York: Routledge, 2009), 146.

49. Vincent Ostrom, Charles M. Tiebout, and Robert Warren, "The Organization of Government in Metropolitan Areas: A Theoretical Inquiry," *American Political Science Review* 55, no. 4 (December 1961): 831–42.

50. For more on the emergence of this school, see Aligica and Boettke, *Challenging Institutional Analysis and Development*.

51. Vincent Ostrom and Michael Dean, "Polycentricity," in *Polycentricity and Local Public Economies: Readings from the Workshop in Political Theory and Policy Analysis*, ed. Michael McGinnis (Ann Arbor: University of Michigan Press, 1999), 52.

52. Ibid., 57.

53. For an overview, see Aligica and Boettke, *Challenging Institutional Analysis and Development*.

54. Elinor Ostrom, *Governing the Commons: The Evolution of Institutions for Collective Action* (Cambridge: Cambridge University Press, 1990), 136. Emphasis original.

55. Barry R. Weingast, "The Economic Role of Political Institutions: Market-Preserving Federalism and Economic Growth," *Journal of Law, Economics, and Organization* 11, no. 1 (February 1995): 3.

56. James Madison, Federalist No. 10, in *The Federalist Papers*, intro. and notes Charles R. Kesler, ed. Clinton Rossiter (New York: Signet Classics, 2003); James Madison, Federalist No. 45, in *The Federalist Papers*, intro. and notes Charles R. Kesler, ed. Clinton Rossiter (New York: Signet Classics, 2003); F. A. Hayek, "The Economic Conditions of Interstate Federalism," in *Individualism and the Economic Order* (Chicago: University of Chicago Press, 1948); Charles M. Tiebout, "A Pure Theory of Local Expenditures," *Journal of Political Economy* 64, no. 5 (October 1956): 416–24; Wallace E. Oates, *Fiscal Federalism* (New York: Harcourt Brace Jovanovich, 1972).

57. William H. Riker, *Federalism: Origin, Operation, Significance* (Little, Brown, 1964), 11.

58. Weingast, "Economic Role of Political Institutions," 4.

59. Richard E. Wagner and Akira Yokoyama, "Polycentrism, Federalism, and Liberty: A Comparative Systems Perspective" (GMU Working Paper in Economics No. 14-10, May 10, 2014).

60. However, lower-level governments competing with one another by offering special privileges to relocating firms would not be market preserving.

61. Michael S. Greve, *The Upside-Down Constitution* (Cambridge, MA: Harvard University Press, 2012).

62. Jerry Ellig, Patrick A. McLaughlin, and John F. Morrall III, "Continuity, Change, and Priorities: The Quality and Use of Regulatory Analysis across US Administrations," *Regulation & Governance* 7, no. 2 (June 2013): 153–73.

63. Jerry Ellig and Christopher J. Conover, "Presidential Priorities, Congressional Control, and the Quality of Regulatory Analysis: An Application to Healthcare and Homeland Security," *Public Choice* 161, no. 3–4 (October 2014): 305–20.

64. Jerry Brito, "Running for Cover: The BRAC Commission as a Model for Federal Spending Reform," *Georgetown Journal of Law & Public Policy* 9 (2011): 131.

65. Ibid., 134.

66. Eileen Norcross and Andrew Biggs, "The Crisis in Public Sector Pension Plans: A Blueprint for Reform in New Jersey" (Mercatus Working Paper, Mercatus Center at George Mason University, Arlington, VA, June 23, 2010); Eileen Norcross, "Pension Reform in Alabama: A Case for Economic Accounting," in *Improving Lives in Alabama: A Vision for Economic Freedom and Prosperity* (Troy, AL: Manuel H. Johnson Center for Political Economy at Troy University, 2014); Eileen Norcross, "A Reality Check on the Public Pension Crisis," *New York Times*, December 5, 2013.

67. Amilcare Puviani, *Teoria della Illusione Finanziaria* (Milan: ISEDI, Istituto Editoriale Internazionale, 1903).

68. Jim Lockwood, "Moody's Views Scranton's $150M Pension Liability as Actually Closer to $250M," *Times-Tribune*, August 9, 2014; Congressional Budget Office, *The Underfunding of State and Local Pension Plans* (Economic and Budget Issue Brief, Washington, DC, May 2011); Daniel Gallagher, "Remarks at Municipal Securities Rulemaking Board's 1st Annual Municipal Securities Regulator Summit" (presentation, Washington, DC, May 29, 2014).

69. Matthew D. Mitchell and Nick Tuszynski, "Institutions and State Spending: An Overview," *Independent Review* 17, no. 1 (Summer 2012): 35–49.

70. Timothy Besley and Anne Case, "Political Institutions and Policy Choices: Evidence from the United States," *Journal of Economic Literature* 41, no. 1 (March 2003): 7–73.

71. W. Mark Crain, *Volatile States: Institutions, Policy, and the Performance of American State Economies* (Ann Arbor: University of Michigan Press, 2003).

72. Matthew D. Mitchell, "TEL It Like It Is: Do State Tax and Expenditure Limits Actually Limit Spending?" (Mercatus Working Paper, Mercatus Center at George Mason University, Arlington, VA, December 6, 2010).

5. The Political Process

1. James M. Buchanan, "The Constitution of Economic Policy," *American Economic Review* 77, no. 3 (June 1987): 246, quoted in *Mainline Economics*, ed. Boettke, Haeffele-Balch, and Storr, 50.

2. Gordon Tullock, *The Vote Motive*, ed. Peter Kurrild-Klitgaard (London: Institute of Economic Affairs, 2006), 44.

3. Christopher J. Coyne, *Doing Bad by Doing Good: Why Humanitarian Action Fails* (Stanford, CA: Stanford Economics and Finance, 2013), xiii–xiv. Benjamin Powell considers another topic that is often talked about in normative terms without any regard to the positive implications of policy—sweatshops. Benjamin Powell, *Out of Poverty: Sweatshops in the Global Economy* (New York: Cambridge University Press, 2014).

4. James M. Buchanan, "Public Choice: Politics without Romance," *Policy* 19, no. 3 (Spring 2003): 13–18.

5. Anthony Downs, *An Economic Theory of Democracy* (New York: Harper and Row, 1957).

6. Chris Cillizza, "People Hate Congress. But Most Incumbents Get Re-elected. What Gives?," *Washington Post*, May 9, 2013.

7. Bryan Caplan, *The Myth of the Rational Voter: Why Democracies Choose Bad Policies*, new ed. (Princeton, NJ: Princeton University Press, 2008).

8. Gert Stulp et al., "Tall Claims? Sense and Nonsense about the Importance of Height of US Presidents," *Leadership Quarterly* 24 (February 2013): 159–171.

9. Alexander Todorov et al., "Inferences of Competence from Faces Predict Election Outcomes," *Science* 308, no. 5728 (June 10, 2005): 1623–26.

10. Pigou, *Economics of Welfare.*

11. Gordon Tullock was the first to point out the externality problem associated with voting. Gordon Tullock, "Problems of Majority Voting," *Journal of Political Economy* 67, no. 6 (December 1959): 571–79. As with private externalities, these political externalities might be internalized if transaction costs were low. But political transaction costs are typically thought to be much higher than private transaction costs. See Daron Acemoglu, "Why Not a Political Coase Theorem? Social Conflict, Commitment, and Politics," *Journal of Comparative Economics* 31, no. 4 (2003): 620; Avinash K. Dixit, *The Making of Economic Policy: A Transaction-Cost Politics Perspective* (Cambridge, MA: MIT Press, 1998), 48–49.

12. Alexandra Wexler, "Bulk of US Sugar Loans Went to Three Companies," *Wall Street Journal,* June 26, 2013.

13. Mancur Olson, *The Logic of Collective Action: Public Goods and the Theory of Groups,* second printing with new preface and appendix, rev. ed. (Cambridge, MA: Harvard University Press, 1965).

14. For a current and highly readable treatment of Olson, see Jonathan Rauch, *Government's End: Why Washington Stopped Working* (New York: PublicAffairs, 1999).

15. The term dates back to David Ricardo's analysis of land rent. David Ricardo, *On the Principles of Political Economy, and Taxation* (London: John Murray, 1817).

16. Though the term *rent-seeking* was coined by economist Anne Krueger, the concept was originally developed by Gordon Tullock; Anne O. Krueger, "The Political Economy of the Rent-Seeking Society," *American Economic Review* 64, no. 3 (1974): 291–303; Gordon Tullock, "The Welfare Costs of Tariffs, Monopolies, and Theft," *Economic Inquiry* 5, no. 3 (June 1967): 224–32.

17. For a discussion of the various ways governments can privilege particular firms or industries, see Mitchell, *Pathology of Privilege.*

18. Ibid., 20.

19. Mitchell, *Pathology of Privilege.*

20. Richard Olney quoted in Milton Friedman and Rose Friedman, *Free to Choose: A Personal Statement* (New York: Harcourt, 1990), 197.

21. George J. Stigler, "The Theory of Economic Regulation," *Bell Journal of Economics and Management Science* 2, no. 1 (Spring 1971): 3.

22. Using more neutral language, Posner called Stigler's idea the "economic theory of regulation," contrasting it with the capture theories of leftist thinkers, such as Kolko. Richard A. Posner, "Theories of Economic Regulation," *Bell Journal of Economics and Management Science* 5, no. 2 (October 1974): 335–58.

23. Ernesto Dal Bó, "Regulatory Capture: A Review," *Oxford Review of Economic Policy* 22, no. 2 (June 2006): 203–25; Randall L. Calvert, "The Value of Biased Information: A Rational Choice Model of Political Advice," *Journal of Politics* 47, no. 2 (June 1985): 530–55.

24. Jordi Blanes i Vidal, Mirko Draca, and Christian Fons-Rosen, "Revolving Door Lobbyists," *American Economic Review* 102, no. 7 (December 2012): 3731–48.

25. Mitchell, *Pathology of Privilege*, 32.

26. Bruce Yandle, "Bootleggers and Baptists: The Education of a Regulatory Economist," *AEI Journal on Government and Society* (June 1983); Adam Smith and Bruce Yandle, *Bootleggers and Baptists: How Economic Forces and Moral Persuasion Interact to Shape Regulatory Politics* (Washington: Cato Institute, 2014).

27. Alyssa Newcomb, "California State Sen. Leland Yee Indicted on Weapons Charges, Was Gun Control Advocate," *ABC News*, March 27, 2014.

28. It is important that other things are equal. Factors such as time of day, whether you've recently eaten, or whether last night was a "big night" might all affect your preference ordering.

29. Arnold A. Weinstein, "Transitivity of Preference: A Comparison among Age Groups," *Journal of Political Economy* 76, no. 2 (March 1968): 307–11; Hinton Bradbury and Karen Ross, "The Effects of Novelty and Choice Materials on the Intransitivity of Preferences of Children and Adults," *Annals of Operations Research* 23, no. 1 (December 1990): 141–59.

30. Duncan Black, "On the Rationale of Group Decision-Making," *Journal of Political Economy* 56, no. 1 (February 1948): 23–34;

Kenneth Joseph Arrow, *Social Choice and Individual Values* (New Haven: Yale University Press, 1951).

31. Voting cycles are especially likely when the decision is "multidimensional" in the sense that it affects more than one thing that voters might care about. For example, a congressional vote to go to war can involve a number of issues simultaneously—national security, tax rates, debt, the nation's reputation, and more. Voting cycles also appear when there are sizeable portions of the electorate with "multi-peaked preferences." For more details, see Dennis C. Mueller, *Public Choice III* (Cambridge: Cambridge University Press, 2003), chapter 5.

32. Interestingly, James Buchanan didn't find voting cycles all that problematic. He pointed out that there might be some value in experimentally adopting one policy, abandoning it, and trying another. James M. Buchanan, "Social Choice, Democracy, and Free Markets," *Journal of Political Economy* 62, no. 2 (April 1954): 114–23.

33. Benjamin Barber extols what he calls "strong democracy," which "can be formally defined as *politics in the participatory mode where conflict is resolved in the absence of an independent ground through a participatory process of ongoing, proximate self-legislation and the creation of a political community capable of transforming dependent, private individuals into free citizens and partial and private interests into public goods.*" Emphasis original. Benjamin R. Barber, *Strong Democracy: Participatory Politics for a New Age* (Berkeley: University of California Press, 2003), 132.

34. Richard D. McKelvey, "Intransitivities in Multidimensional Voting Models and Some Implications for Agenda Control," *Journal of Economic Theory* 12, no. 3 (June 1976): 472–82.

35. Smith, *Wealth of Nations*, book I, chapter 2.

36. Buchanan, "Constitution of Economic Policy," quoted in *Mainline Economics*, ed. Boettke, Haeffele-Balch, and Storr, 53; Knut Wicksell, "A New Principle of Just Taxation," in *Classics in the Theory of Public Finance*, ed. Richard Musgrave and Alan Peacock (London: Macmillan, 1958), 72–118.

37. Buchanan, "Constitution of Economic Policy," quoted in *Mainline Economics*, ed. Boettke, Haeffele-Balch, and Storr, 50.

38. Ibid., quoted in *Mainline Economics*, ed. Boettke, Haeffele-Balch, and Storr, 51.

39. In his subsequent study, Olson repeatedly stresses that he is not advocating a "monocausal" theory. See, for example, Mancur Olson, *The Rise and Decline of Nations: Economic Growth, Stagflation, and Social Rigidities* (New Haven: Yale University Press, 1982), 15.

40. Both Hayek and Keynes believed that academic ideas had great sway over institutions and policy, especially in the long run. For more on this theory, see the insightful study by Edward López and Wayne Leighton, *Madmen, Intellectuals, and Academic Scribblers: The Economic Engine of Political Change* (Stanford, CA: Stanford University Press, 2012). The Federal Trade Commission's advocacy efforts to persuade state and local governments to remove barriers to entry seem designed to raise the cost of bad decisions. Todd J. Zywicki, James C. Cooper, and Paul A. Pautler, "Theory and Practice of Competition Advocacy at the FTC," *Antitrust Law Journal* 72, no. 3 (2005): 1091–112.

41. Jerry Ellig and Richard Williams, "Reforming Regulatory Analysis, Review, and Oversight: A Guide for the Perplexed" (Mercatus Working Paper, Mercatus Center at George Mason University, Arlington, VA, August 13, 2014); John F. Morrall III and James Broughel, "The Role of Regulatory Impact Analysis in Federal Rulemaking" (Mercatus Research, Mercatus Center at George Mason University, Arlington, VA, April 10, 2014).

42. Morrall III and Broughel, "The Role of Regulatory Impact Analysis in Federal Rulemaking," 1–4.

43. Buchanan, *Cost and Choice*.

44. Omar Al-Ubaydli and Patrick A. McLaughlin, "RegData: A Numerical Database on Industry-Specific Regulations for All United States Industries and Federal Regulations, 1997–2012," *Regulation & Governance* (2015).

45. Antony Davies, "Regulation and Productivity" (Mercatus Research, Mercatus Center at George Mason University, Arlington, VA, May 8, 2014).

46. James Bailey and Diana Thomas, "Regulating Away Competition: The Effect of Regulation on Entrepreneurship and Employment" (Mercatus Working Paper, Mercatus Center at George Mason University, Arlington, VA, September 2015).

47. Patrick A. McLaughlin, Matthew D. Mitchell, and Thomas Stratmann, "Does Regulation Enhance or Inhibit Turnover of Firms by Industry?" (Mercatus Working Paper, Mercatus Center at George Mason University, Arlington, VA, forthcoming).

48. Jerry Brito and Jerry Ellig, "Video Franchising" (Public Interest Comment, Mercatus Center at George Mason University, Arlington, VA, February 13, 2006); Jerry Brito and Jerry Ellig, "Video Killed the Franchise Star: The Consumer Cost of Cable Franchising and Proposed Policy Alternatives," *Journal on Telecommunications & High Technology Law* 5 (2006): 199.

49. Veronique de Rugy, "The Biggest Beneficiaries of the Ex-Im Bank" (Chart, Mercatus Center at George Mason University, Arlington, VA, April 29, 2014).

50. Matthew D. Mitchell, "Ex-Im's Deadweight Loss," *Neighborhood Effects*, Mercatus Center at George Mason University, August 6, 2014.

51. For an overview of some of this work, see "Export-Import Bank," Mercatus Center at George Mason University, accessed October 26, 2016, https://www.mercatus.org/tags/export -import-bank.

52. Milton Friedman, *A Theory of the Consumption Function* (1957; Pickle Partners Publishing, 2016).

53. John Taylor, "An Empirical Analysis of the Revival of Fiscal Activism in the 2000s," *Journal of Economic Literature* 49, no. 3 (2011): 686–702; For a short summary of Taylor's research, see Nita Ghei, "The Unstimulated Economy," *Washington Times*, July 8, 2011.

54. John Maynard Keynes, "The International Control of Raw Materials," in *The Collected Writings of John Maynard Keynes*, vol. 27, ed. Elizabeth Johnson and Donald Moggridge (1942; Cambridge: Cambridge University Press, 2012), 122.

55. Lawrence Summers, "The State of the US Economy" (Brookings Institution Forum, Washington, DC, December 18, 2007).

56. Veronique de Rugy and Matthew D. Mitchell, "Would More Infrastructure Spending Stimulate the Economy?" (Mercatus Working Paper, Mercatus Center at George Mason University, Arlington, VA, September 12, 2011), 4.

57. Committee on Appropriations, US House of Representatives, "Summary: American Recovery and Reinvestment," February 13, 2009.

58. Government Accountability Office, "Recovery Act: Funding Used for Transportation Infrastructure Projects, but Some Requirements Proved Challenging" (GAO Report 11-600, June 29, 2011).

59. Veronique de Rugy, "Stimulus Facts: Period 2" (Mercatus Working Paper, Mercatus Center at George Mason University, Arlington, VA, April 7, 2010).

60. Jason Reifler and Jeffrey Lazarus, "Partisanship and Policy Priorities in the Distribution of Economic Stimulus Funds" (SSRN Scholarly Paper, September 1, 2010); Robert P. Inman, "States in Fiscal Distress," *Federal Reserve Bank of Saint Louis Regional Economic Development* 6, no. 1 (October 2010): 65–80.

61. Garett Jones and Daniel Rothschild, "Did Stimulus Dollars Hire the Unemployed? Answers to Questions about the American Recovery and Reinvestment Act" (Mercatus Working Paper, Mercatus Center at George Mason University, Arlington, VA, August 30, 2011).

62. Ibid., 1.

63. Russell S. Sobel and George R. Crowley, "Do Intergovernmental Grants Create Ratchets in State and Local Taxes? Testing the Friedman-Sanford Hypothesis" (Mercatus Working Paper No. 10-51, Mercatus Center at George Mason University, Arlington, VA, August 2010).

64. Keynes, *Collected Writings of John Maynard Keynes.*

65. Jason E. Taylor and Andrea Castillo, "'Timely, Targeted, and Temporary?' An Analysis of Government Expansions over the Past Century" (Mercatus Research, Mercatus Center at George Mason University, Arlington, VA, January 2014), 29.

66. Barro and Redlick, for example, find that when one takes into account the tax multiplier, the balanced budget multiplier for defense spending is negative. Robert J. Barro and Charles J. Redlick, "Macroeconomic Effects from Government Purchases and Taxes" (Mercatus Working Paper, Mercatus Center at George Mason University, Arlington, VA, July 2010).

67. Matthew D. Mitchell, "What Can Government Do to Create Jobs?" (Testimony before the House Committee on Education and Workforce, Mercatus Center at George Mason University, February 1, 2012).

6. A Liberal Program That Appeals to the Imagination

1. Vernon L. Smith, "Constructivist and Ecological Rationality in Economics," *American Economic Review* 93, no. 3

(June 2003): 465, quoted in *Mainline Economics*, ed. Boettke, Haeffele-Balch, and Storr, 104.

2. Hayek, "Intellectuals and Socialism," 432.

3. Buchanan, "Constitution of Economic Policy," 250, quoted in *Mainline Economics*, ed. Boettke, Haeffele-Balch, and Storr, 59.

4. Stigler, "Theory of Economic Regulation"; Mark Green and Ralph Nader, "Economic Regulation vs. Competition: Uncle Sam the Monopoly Man," *Yale Law Journal* 82, no. 5 (April 1973): 871–89.

5. Gene Smiley, *The American Economy in the Twentieth Century* (Cincinnati, OH: South-Western Publishing, 1993), 218.

6. James M. Buchanan, "Notes on Hayek—Miami, 15 February, 1970," *Review of Austrian Economics* 28, no. 3 (September 2015): 257–60.

7. The occasion for these remarks was an address that Hayek delivered at the University of Chicago in October 1963. F. A. Hayek, "The Economics of the 1930s as Seen from London," in *The Collected Works of F. A. Hayek, Vol. 9, Contra Keynes and Cambridge: Essays, Correspondence*, ed. Bruce Caldwell (Chicago: University of Chicago Press, 1995), 56.

8. Arnold Kling, "So You Want to Be a Masonomist," *TCS Daily*, October 17, 2007.

9. F. A. Hayek, "F. A. Hayek on Social Evolution and the Origins of Tradition" (paper presented at George Mason University, November 22, 1983).

10. Peter J. Boettke and Rosolino A. Candela, "Alchian, Buchanan, and Coase: A Neglected Branch of Chicago Price Theory," *Man and the Economy* 1, no. 2 (December 2014): 189–208.

11. James M. Buchanan, "Chicago School Thinking: Old and New," YouTube video, from a speech at University of Richmond on June 20, 2010, posted June 22, 2010.

12. Boettke and Candela, "Alchian, Buchanan, and Coase."

13. Both history of economic thought and economic history were required courses in the economics PhD curriculum when the program was established. Though this has since changed, these fields remain strong aspects of Mason's research and graduate education.

14. Jennifer Howard, "Academic Center Offers Peer Review, Face to Face," *Chronicle of Higher Education*, March 3, 2014.

15. See, for example, the following: Elinor Ostrom and Vincent Ostrom, "Rethinking Institutional Analysis: Interviews with Vincent and Elinor Ostrom," interview by Paul Dragos Aligica (Mercatus Center at George Mason University, Arlington, VA, November 7, 2003); Aligica and Boettke, *Challenging Institutional Analysis and Development*; Peter J. Boettke, "Introduction," in "Polycentric Political Economy: A Festschrift for Elinor and Vincent Ostrom," Special issue, *Journal of Economic Behavior & organization* 57, no. 2 (June 2005): 141–43. The last is the published proceedings of a conference held at the Mercatus Center in 2003.

16. Smith, "Constructivist and Ecological Rationality in Economics," quoted in *Mainline Economics*, ed. Boettke, Haeffele-Balch, and Storr.

17. F. A. Hayek, "The Dilemma of Specialization," in *The State of the Social Sciences*, ed. Leonard D. White (Chicago: University of Chicago Press, 1956), 463.

18. Justin Lafreniere, "'Economics with Attitude' Gets High Ranking," *News at Mason*, George Mason University, February 10, 2014.

19. Each of these "straw man" arguments for free enterprise is built and then handily dispatched in Paul Krugman, "How Did Economists Get It So Wrong?," *New York Times Magazine*, September 2, 2009.

20. James M. Buchanan, "The Thomas Jefferson Center for Studies in Political Economy," *University of Virginia News Letter* 35, no. 2 (October 15, 1958).

21. As Hayek put it, "Individual freedom, wherever it has existed, has been largely the product of a prevailing respect for such principles which, however, have never been fully articulated in constitutional documents." F. A. Hayek, "Principles or Expediency?," in *Toward Liberty: Essays in Honor of Ludwig von Mises on the Occasion of His 90th Birthday*, vol.1, ed. F. A. Hayek et al. (Menlo Park CA: Institute for Humane Studies, 1971).

BIBLIOGRAPHY

Abrams, Burton A. "How Richard Nixon Pressured Arthur Burns: Evidence from the Nixon Tapes." *Journal of Economic Perspectives* 20, no. 4 (2006): 177–88.

Acemoglu, Daron. "Why Not a Political Coase Theorem? Social Conflict, Commitment, and Politics." *Journal of Comparative Economics* 31, no. 4 (2003): 620–52.

Acemoglu, Daron, Simon Johnson, and James A. Robinson. "The Colonial Origins of Comparative Development: An Empirical Investigation." *American Economic Review* 91, no. 5 (December 2001): 1369–401.

Acemoglu, Daron, and James Robinson. *Why Nations Fail: The Origins of Power, Prosperity, and Poverty.* New York: Crown Business, 2012.

Adams, John. *Novanglus, Thoughts on Government, Defence of the Constitution.* Vol. 4 of *The Works of John Adams, Second President of the United States: With a Life of the Author, Notes and Illustrations, by His Grandson Charles Francis Adams.* Boston, MA: Little, Brown, 1856.

Ades, Alberto F., and Edward L. Glaeser. "Evidence on Growth, Increasing Returns, and the Extent of the Market." *Quarterly Journal of Economics* 114, no. 3 (1999): 1025–45.

Akerlof, George A. "The Market for 'Lemons': Quality Uncertainty and the Market Mechanism." *Quarterly Journal of Economics* 84, no. 3 (August 1970): 488–500.

Alchian, Armen A. "Property Rights." In *The Concise Encyclopedia of Economics.* Edited by David Henderson. Indianapolis: Liberty Fund, 2008.

———. "Some Economics of Property Rights." *Il Politico* 30, no. 4 (December 1965): 816–29.

———. "Uncertainty, Evolution, and Economic Theory." *Journal of Political Economy* 58, no. 3 (June 1950): 211–21.

Alchian, Armen A., and William R. Allen. *Exchange and Production: Competition, Coordination, and Control.* 3rd ed. Belmont, CA: Wadsworth Publishing, 1983.

Alchian, Armen A., and Harold Demsetz. "Production, Information Costs, and Economic Organization." *American Economic Review* 62, no. 5 (December 1972): 777–95.

Aligica, Paul Dragos, and Peter J. Boettke. *Challenging Institutional Analysis and Development: The Bloomington School*. New York: Routledge, 2009.

Al-Ubaydli, Omar, Daniel Houser, John Nye, Maria Pia Paganelli, and Xiaofei Sophia Pan. "The Causal Effect of Market Priming on Trust: An Experimental Investigation Using Randomized Control." *PLoS ONE* 8, no. 3 (March 5, 2013): e55968.

Angrist, Joshua D., and Alan B. Krueger. "Empirical Strategies in Labor Economics." Vol. 3, Part A, of *Handbook of Labor Economics*, edited by Orley Ashenfelter and David Card, 1277–366. Amsterdam: Elsevier, 1999.

Angrist, Joshua D., and Victor Lavy. "Using Maimonides' Rule to Estimate the Effect of Class Size on Scholastic Achievement." *Quarterly Journal of Economics* 114, no. 2 (1999): 533–75.

Angrist, Joshua D., and Jörn-Steffen Pischke. "The Credibility Revolution in Empirical Economics: How Better Research Design Is Taking the Con Out of Econometrics." NBER Working Paper No. 15794, National Bureau of Economic Research, March 2010.

Arrow, Kenneth Joseph. *Social Choice and Individual Values*. New Haven: Yale University Press, 1951.

Bagehot, Walter. *Lombard Street: A Description of the Money Market*. 1873. Lexington, KY: CreateSpace Independent Publishing Platform, 2013.

Bailey, James, and Diana W. Thomas. "Regulating Away Competition: The Effect of Regulation on Entrepreneurship and Employment." Mercatus Working Paper, Mercatus Center at George Mason University, Arlington, VA, September 2015.

Barber, Benjamin R. *Strong Democracy: Participatory Politics for a New Age*. Berkeley: University of California Press, 2004.

Barnett, Randy E. *Restoring the Lost Constitution: The Presumption of Liberty*. Princeton, NJ: Princeton University Press, 2013.

Barro, Robert J., and Charles J. Redlick. "Macroeconomic Effects from Government Purchases and Taxes." Mercatus Working Paper, Mercatus Center at George Mason University, Arlington, VA, July 2010.

Bastiat, Frédéric. *Economic Sophisms*. Translated and edited by Arthur Goddard. 1845. Irvington-on-Hudson, NY: Foundation for Economic Education, 1996.

———. *The Law*. Translated by Dean Russell. 1850. Irvington-on-Hudson, NY: Foundation for Economic Education, 1998.

———. "What Is Seen and What Is Not Seen." In *Selected Essays on Political Economy*. Translated by Seymour Cain. 1848. Irvington-on-Hudson, NY: Foundation for Economic Education, 1995.

Bates, Karen Grigsby. "Condiment Detente: Sriracha Plant to Stay in California City." NPR. May 29, 2014.

Baumol, William J. "Entrepreneurship: Productive, Unproductive, and Destructive." *Journal of Political Economy* 98, no. 5 (October 1990): 893–921.

Besley, Timothy, and Anne Case. "Political Institutions and Policy Choices: Evidence from the United States." *Journal of Economic Literature* 41, no. 1 (March 2003): 7–73.

Bicchieri, Cristina. *The Grammar of Society: The Nature and Dynamics of Social Norms*. Cambridge: Cambridge University Press, 2006.

Black, Duncan. "On the Rationale of Group Decision-Making." *Journal of Political Economy* 56, no. 1 (February 1948): 23–34.

Blanes i Vidal, Jordi, Mirko Draca, and Christian Fons-Rosen. "Revolving Door Lobbyists." *American Economic Review* 102, no. 7 (December 2012): 3731–48.

Bloom, David E., and Jeffrey D. Sachs. "Geography, Demography, and Economic Growth in Africa." *Brookings Papers on Economic Activity* 29, no. 2 (1998): 207–96.

Boettke, Peter J. "Austrian School of Economics." In *The Concise Encyclopedia of Economics*. Edited by David Henderson. Indianapolis: Liberty Fund, 2008.

———. *Calculation and Coordination: Essays on Socialism and Transitional Political Economy*. London: Routledge, 2001.

———. "Introduction." In "Polycentric Political Economy: A Festschrift for Elinor and Vincent Ostrom." Special issue, *Journal of Economic Behavior and* 57, no. 2 (June 2005): 141–43.

———. "Introduction." In *Handbook on Contemporary Austrian Economics*. Cheltenham, UK: Edward Elgar, 2010.

———. "Liberty vs. Power in Economic Policy in the 20th and 21st Centuries." *Journal of Private Enterprise* 22, no. 2 (Spring 2007): 7–36.

———. *Living Economics: Yesterday, Today, and Tomorrow*. Oakland, CA: Independent Institute, 2012.

———, ed. *Socialism and the Market: The Socialist Calculation Debate Revisited*. London: Routledge, 2000.

Boettke, Peter J., and Rosolino A. Candela. "Alchian, Buchanan, and Coase: A Neglected Branch of Chicago Price Theory." *Man and the Economy* 1, no. 2 (December 2014): 189–208.

Boettke, Peter J., and Christopher J. Coyne. "The Debt-Inflation Cycle and the Global Financial Crisis." *Global Policy* 2, no. 2 (May 2011): 184–89.

Boettke, Peter J., Christopher J. Coyne, and Peter T. Leeson. "Institutional Stickiness and the New Development Economics." *American Journal of Economics and Sociology* 67, no. 2 (April 2008): 331–58.

Boettke, Peter J., Stefanie Haeffele-Balch, and Virgil Henry Storr, eds. *Mainline Economics: Six Nobel Lectures in the Tradition of Adam Smith.* Arlington, VA: Mercatus Center at George Mason University, 2016.

Boudreaux, Donald J., Robert Lawson, Roger Meiners, Andrew Morriss, Liya Palagashvili, Russell Sobel, and Wayne Crews. *What America's Decline in Economic Freedom Means for Entrepreneurship and Prosperity.* Arlington, VA: Mercatus Center at George Mason University, 2015.

Bradbury, Hinton, and Karen Ross. "The Effects of Novelty and Choice Materials on the Intransitivity of Preferences of Children and Adults." *Annals of Operations Research* 23, no. 1 (December 1990): 141–59.

Brito, Jerry. "Running for Cover: The BRAC Commission as a Model for Federal Spending Reform." *Georgetown Journal of Law & Public Policy* 9 (2011): 131.

Brito, Jerry, and Jerry Ellig. "Video Franchising." Public Interest Comment, Mercatus Center at George Mason University, Arlington, VA, February 13, 2006.

———. "Video Killed the Franchise Star: The Consumer Cost of Cable Franchising and Proposed Policy Alternatives." *Journal on Telecommunications & High Technology Law* 5 (2006): 199.

Buchanan, James M. "Chicago School Thinking: Old and New." Filmed June 20, 2010. YouTube video. Speech at University of Richmond. Posted June 22, 2010.

———. "The Constitution of Economic Policy." *American Economic Review* 77, no. 3 (June 1987). Quoted in *Mainline Economics: Six Nobel Lectures in the Tradition of Adam Smith.* Edited by Peter J. Boettke, Stefanie Haeffele-Balch, and Virgil Henry Storr. Arlington, VA: Mercatus Center at George Mason University, 2016.

———. *Cost and Choice: An Inquiry in Economic Theory.* Indianapolis: Liberty Fund, 1969.

———. "The Domain of Constitutional Economics." *Constitutional Political Economy* 1, no. 1 (December 1990): 1–18.

———. *The Limits of Liberty: Between Anarchy and Leviathan*. Chicago: University of Chicago Press, 1975.

———. "Notes on Hayek—Miami, 15 February, 1979." *Review of Austrian Economics* 28, no. 3 (September 2015): 257–60.

———. "Public Choice: Politics without Romance." *Policy* 19, no. 3 (Spring 2003): 13–18.

———. "Social Choice, Democracy, and Free Markets." *Journal of Political Economy* 62, no. 2 (April 1954): 114–23.

———. "The Thomas Jefferson Center for Studies in Political Economy." *The University of Virginia News Letter* 35, no. 2 (October 15, 1958).

———. "What Should Economists Do?" *Southern Economic Journal* 30, no. 3 (January 1964): 213–22.

Buchanan, James M., and Gordon Tullock. *The Calculus of Consent: Logical Foundations of Constitutional Democracy*. Ann Arbor: University of Michigan Press, 1962.

Buchanan, James M., and Richard E. Wagner. *Democracy in Deficit: The Political Legacy of Lord Keynes*. Indianapolis: Liberty Fund, 1977.

Calvert, Randall L. "The Value of Biased Information: A Rational Choice Model of Political Advice." *Journal of Politics* 47, no. 2 (June 1985): 530–55.

Caplan, Bryan. *The Myth of the Rational Voter: Why Democracies Choose Bad Policies*. New ed. Princeton, NJ: Princeton University Press, 2008.

Chamlee-Wright, Emily, and Virgil Henry Storr. "The Role of Social Entrepreneurship in Post-Katrina Community Recovery." In *The Political Economy of Hurricane Katrina and Community Rebound*. Edited by Emily Chamlee-Wright and Virgil Henry Storr. Cheltenham, UK: Edward Elgar, 2010.

Cillizza, Chris. "People Hate Congress. But Most Incumbents Get Re-elected. What Gives?" *Washington Post*, May 9, 2013.

Clark, Gregory. *A Farewell to Alms: A Brief Economic History of the World*. Princeton, NJ: Princeton University Press, 2009.

Coase, Ronald H. "The Federal Communications Commission." *Journal of Law and Economics* 2 (October 1959): 1–40.

———. "The Institutional Structure of Production." *American Economic Review* 82, no. 4 (September 1992). Quoted in *Mainline Economics: Six Nobel Lectures in the Tradition of Adam Smith*. Edited by Peter J. Boettke, Stefanie Haeffele-Balch, and Virgil Henry Storr. Arlington, VA: Mercatus Center at George Mason University, 2016.

———. "The Nature of the Firm." *Economica* 4, no. 16 (1937): 386–405.

———. "The Problem of Social Cost." *Journal of Law and Economics* 3 (October 1960): 1–44.

Committee on Appropriations, US House of Representatives. "Summary: American Recovery and Reinvestment." February 13, 2009.

Congressional Budget Office. *The Underfunding of State and Local Pension Plans.* Economic and Budget Issue Brief, Washington, DC, May 2011.

Cowen, Tyler. *The Great Stagnation: How America Ate All the Low-Hanging Fruit of Modern History, Got Sick, and Will (Eventually) Feel Better.* New York: Dutton, 2011.

———. "Public Goods and Externalities." In *The Concise Encyclopedia of Economics.* Edited by David Henderson. Indianapolis: Liberty Fund, 1993.

Cowen, Tyler, and Alexander T. Tabarrok. *Modern Principles of Economics.* New York: Worth Publishers, 2009.

Coyne, Christopher J. *Doing Bad by Doing Good: Why Humanitarian Action Fails.* Stanford, CA: Stanford University Press, 2013.

Crain, W. Mark. *Volatile States: Institutions, Policy, and the Performance of American State Economies.* Ann Arbor: University of Michigan Press, 2003.

Dahlman, Carl J. "The Problem of Externality." *Journal of Law and Economics* 22, no. 1 (1979): 141–62.

Dal Bó, Ernesto. "Regulatory Capture: A Review." *Oxford Review of Economic Policy* 22, no. 2 (June 2006): 203–25.

Davies, Antony. "Regulation and Productivity." Mercatus Research, Mercatus Center at George Mason University, Arlington, VA, May 8, 2014.

Deary, Ian J. *Intelligence: A Very Short Introduction.* Oxford: Oxford University Press, 2001.

Decker, Ryan, John Haltiwanger, Ron Jarmin, and Javier Miranda. "The Role of Entrepreneurship in US Job Creation and Economic Dynamism." *Journal of Economic Perspectives* 28, no. 3 (2014): 3–24.

De Long, J. Bradford, and Andrei Shleifer. "Princes and Merchants: European City Growth before the Industrial Revolution." *Journal of Law and Economics* 36, no. 2 (October 1993): 671–702.

Demsetz, Harold. "Toward a Theory of Property Rights." *American Economic Review* 57, no. 2 (May 1967): 347–59.

de Rugy, Veronique. "The Biggest Beneficiaries of the Ex-Im Bank." Chart, Mercatus Center at George Mason University, Arlington, VA, April 29, 2014.

———. "Stimulus Facts: Period 2." Mercatus Working Paper, Mercatus Center at George Mason University, Arlington, VA, April 7, 2010.

de Rugy, Veronique, and Matthew D. Mitchell. "Would More Infrastructure Spending Stimulate the Economy?" Mercatus Working Paper, Mercatus Center at George Mason University, Arlington, VA, September 12, 2011.

Diamond, Jared. *Guns, Germs, and Steel: The Fates of Human Societies.* New York: W. W. Norton, 1999.

Diener, Ed, Marissa Diener, and Carol Diener. "Factors Predicting the Subjective Well-Being of Nations." In *Culture and Well-Being,* edited by Edward Diener, 43–70. Dordrecht, Netherlands: Springer, 2009.

Dixit, Avinash K. *The Making of Economic Policy: A Transaction-Cost Politics Perspective.* Cambridge, MA: MIT Press, 1998.

Donohue, John J., and Justin Wolfers. "Uses and Abuses of Empirical Evidence in the Death Penalty Debate." *Stanford Law Review* 58, no. 3 (September 2005): 791.

Doucouliagos, Chris, and Mehmet Ali Ulubasoglu. "Economic Freedom and Economic Growth: Does Specification Make a Difference?" *European Journal of Political Economy* 22, no. 1 (March 2006): 60–81.

Downs, Anthony. *An Economic Theory of Democracy.* New York: Harper and Row, 1957.

Duggan, Mark, and Steven D. Levitt. "Winning Isn't Everything: Corruption in Sumo Wrestling." *American Economic Review* 92, no. 5 (December 2002): 1594–605.

Easterlin, Richard A. "Does Economic Growth Improve the Human Lot? Some Empirical Evidence." In *Nations and Households in Economic Growth: Essays in Honour of Moses Abramovitz.* Edited by P. A. David and Melvin W. Reder. New York: Academic Press Inc, 1974.

Easterly, William, and Ross Levine. "Tropics, Germs, and Crops: How Endowments Influence Economic Development." *Journal of Monetary Economics* 50, no. 1 (January 2003): 3–39.

Ehrlich, Isaac. "The Deterrent Effect of Capital Punishment: A Question of Life and Death." *American Economic Review* 65, no. 3 (June 1975): 397–417.

Ellickson, Robert. *Order without Law: How Neighbors Settle Disputes.* Cambridge, MA: Harvard University Press, 1994.

Ellig, Jerry. "Railroad Deregulation and Consumer Welfare." *Journal of Regulatory Economics* 21, no. 2 (2002): 143–67.

Ellig, Jerry, and Christopher J. Conover. "Presidential Priorities, Congressional Control, and the Quality of Regulatory Analysis: An Application to Healthcare and Homeland Security." *Public Choice* 161, no. 3–4 (October 2014): 305–20.

Ellig, Jerry, Patrick A. McLaughlin, and John F. Morrall III. "Continuity, Change, and Priorities: The Quality and Use of Regulatory Analysis across US Administrations." *Regulation & Governance* 7, no. 2 (June 2013): 153–73.

Ellig, Jerry, and Richard Williams. "Reforming Regulatory Analysis, Review, and Oversight: A Guide for the Perplexed." Mercatus Working Paper, Mercatus Center at George Mason University, Arlington, VA, August 13, 2014.

Engerman, Stanley L., and Kenneth L. Sokoloff. "Factor Endowments, Inequality, and Paths of Development among New World Economics." NBER Working Paper No. 9259, National Bureau of Economic Research, October 2002.

"Export-Import Bank." Mercatus Center at George Mason University. Accessed October 26, 2016. https://www.mercatus.org/tags /export-import-bank.

Ferguson, Adam. *An Essay on the History of Civil Society.* 5th ed. London: T. Cadell, 1782.

Fisher, Franklin M. *The Identification Problem in Econometrics.* Illus. ed. Huntington, NY: Krieger, 1966.

Fogel, Robert William. *The Escape from Hunger and Premature Death, 1700–2100: Europe, America, and the Third World.* Cambridge: Cambridge University Press, 2004.

Friedman, Benjamin M. *The Moral Consequences of Economic Growth.* New York: Vintage, 2006.

Friedman, Milton. *Capitalism and Freedom.* 40th anniversary ed. Chicago: University of Chicago Press, 2002.

———. "The Fed's Thermostat." *Wall Street Journal,* August 19, 2003.

———. *The Optimum Quantity of Money.* Rev. ed. Edited by Michael D. Bordo. New Brunswick, NJ: Aldine Transaction, 2005.

———. *A Theory of the Consumption Function.* 1957. Pickle Partners Publishing, 2016.

Friedman, Milton, and Rose Friedman. *Free to Choose: A Personal Statement.* New York: Harcourt, 1990.

Fukuda-Parr, Sakiko, et al. *Human Development Report 2004: Cultural Liberty in Today's Diverse World.* New York: United Nations Development Programme, 2004.

Gallagher, Daniel. "Remarks at Municipal Securities Rulemaking Board's 1st Annual Municipal Securities Regulator Summit." Presentation, Washington, DC, May 29, 2014.

Gallup, John Luke, and Jeffrey D. Sachs. "The Economic Burden of Malaria." *American Journal of Tropical Medicine and Hygiene* 64, no. 1–2, suppl (February 2001): 85–96.

Gertler, Paul, Manisha Shah, and Stefano M. Bertozzi. "Risky Business: The Market for Unprotected Commercial Sex." *Journal of Political Economy* 113, no. 3 (June 2005): 518–50.

Ghei, Nita. "The Unstimulated Economy." *Washington Times*, July 8, 2011.

Glaeser, Edward L., Rafael La Porta, Florencio Lopez-de-Silanes, and Andrei Shleifer. "Do Institutions Cause Growth?" *Journal of Economic Growth* 9, no. 3 (September 2004): 271–303.

Government Accountability Office. "Recovery Act: Funding Used for Transportation Infrastructure Projects, but Some Requirements Proved Challenging." GAO Report 11-600, June 29, 2011.

Green, Mark, and Ralph Nader. "Economic Regulation vs. Competition: Uncle Sam the Monopoly Man." *Yale Law Journal* 82, no. 5 (April 1973): 871–89.

Greve, Michael S. *The Upside-Down Constitution*. Cambridge, MA: Harvard University Press, 2012.

Gwartney, James, Robert A. Lawson, and Joshua Hall. *Economic Freedom of the World, 2013 Annual Report*. Vancouver, Canada: Fraser Institute, 2013.

Hagerty, Michael R., and Ruut Veenhoven. "Wealth and Happiness Revisited: Growing Wealth of Nations *Does* Go with Greater Happiness." *Social Indicators Research* 64, no. 1 (2003): 1–27.

Hall, Joshua C., and Robert A. Lawson. "Economic Freedom of the World: An Accounting of the Literature." *Contemporary Economic Policy* 32, no. 1 (2014): 1–19.

Hall, Robert E., and Charles I. Jones. "Why Do Some Countries Produce So Much More Output per Worker Than Others?" *Quarterly Journal of Economics* 114, no. 1 (February 1999): 83–116.

Hardin, Garrett. "The Tragedy of the Commons." *Science* 162, no. 3859 (December 1968): 1243–48.

Harford, Tim. "The Economics of Trust." *Forbes*, November 3, 2006.

Hayek, F. A. "Armen A. Alchian Interviews Friedrich A. Hayek (Part I)." *The Hayek Interviews: Alive and Influential*, video series, November 11, 1978.

———. "Competition as a Discovery Procedure." Translated by Marcellus S. Snow. *Quarterly Journal of Austrian Economics* 5, no. 3 (Fall 2002): 9–23.

———. *The Constitution of Liberty*. Chicago: University of Chicago Press, 1960.

———. "The Dilemma of Specialization." In *The State of the Social Sciences*, edited by Leonard D. White, 463. Chicago: University of Chicago Press, 1956.

———. "The Economic Conditions of Interstate Federalism." 1939. In *Individualism and Economic Order*. Chicago: University of Chicago Press, 1948.

———. "The Economics of the 1930s as Seen from London." In *The Collected Works of F. A. Hayek*. Vol. 9. *Contra Keynes and Cambridge: Essays, Correspondence*, edited by Bruce Caldwell, 49–63. Chicago: University of Chicago Press, 1995.

———. "F. A. Hayek on Social Evolution and the Origins of Tradition." Paper presented at George Mason University, November 22, 1983.

———. *Full Employment at Any Price?* London: Transatlantic Arts, 1975.

———. "The Intellectuals and Socialism." *University of Chicago Law Review* 16, no. 3 (Spring 1949): 417–33.

———. *Law, Legislation and Liberty, Volume 2: The Mirage of Social Justice*. Chicago: University of Chicago Press, 1978.

———. "The Meaning of Competition." In *Individualism and Economic Order*. Reissue ed. Chicago: University of Chicago Press, 1996.

———. "The Pretense of Knowledge." *American Economic Review* 79, no. 6 (December 1989). Quoted in *Mainline Economics: Six Nobel Lectures in the Tradition of Adam Smith*. Edited by Peter J. Boettke, Stefanie Haeffele-Balch, and Virgil Henry Storr. Arlington, VA: Mercatus Center at George Mason University, 2016.

———. *Prices and Production*. 2nd ed. London: Routledge, 1932.

———. "Principles or Expediency?" In vol. 1 of *Toward Liberty: Essays in Honor of Ludwig von Mises on the Occasion of His 90th Birthday*. Edited by F. A. Hayek, Henry Hazlitt, Leonard E. Read, Gustavo R. Velasco, and Floyd Arthur Harper. Menlo Park, CA: Institute for Humane Studies, 1971.

———. *The Road to Serfdom: Text and Documents—The Definitive Edition*. Edited by Bruce Caldwell. Chicago: University of Chicago Press, 1944.

———. "The Use of Knowledge in Society." *American Economic Review* 35, no. 4 (September 1945): 519–30.

Higgs, Robert. *Crisis and Leviathan: Critical Episodes in the Growth of American Government.* 25th anniversary ed. 1987. Oakland, CA: Independent Institute, 2013.

Horwitz, Steven. "Making Hurricane Response More Effective: Lessons from the Private Sector and the Coast Guard during Katrina." In *The Political Economy of Hurricane Katrina and Community Rebound.* Edited by Emily Chamlee-Wright and Virgil Henry Storr. Cheltenham, UK: Edward Elgar, 2010.

Horwitz, Steven, and Peter J. Boettke. *The House That Uncle Sam Built: The Untold Story of the Great Recession of 2008.* Irvington-on-Hudson, NY: Foundation for Economic Education, 2009.

Howard, Jennifer. "Academic Center Offers Peer Review, Face to Face." *The Chronicle of Higher Education,* March 3, 2014.

Hume, David. *Essays: Moral, Political, and Literary.* Rev. ed. Indianapolis: Liberty Fund, 1985.

———. *A Treatise of Human Nature by David Hume, Reprinted from the Original Edition in Three Volumes and Edited, with an Analytical Index, by L. A. Selby-Bigge, M.A.* Oxford: Clarendon Press, 1896. First published 1739.

Inglehart, Ronald. *Culture Shift in Advanced Industrial Society.* Princeton, NJ: Princeton University Press, 1990.

Inglehart, Ronald, and Hans-Dieter Klingemann. "Genes, Culture, Democracy, and Happiness." In *Culture and Subjective Well-Being.* Edited by Edward Diener and Eunkook M. Suh. Reprint, Cambridge, MA: Bradford Books, 2003.

Inman, Robert P. "States in Fiscal Distress." *Federal Reserve Bank of Saint Louis Regional Economic Development* 6, no. 1 (October 2010): 65–80.

Jefferson, Thomas. *The Works of Thomas Jefferson, Vol. 5 (Correspondence 1786–1789).* Edited by Paul Leicester Ford. Federal ed. New York: G. P. Putnam's Sons, 1904.

Jones, Garett, and Daniel M. Rothschild. "Did Stimulus Dollars Hire the Unemployed? Answers to Questions about the American Recovery and Reinvestment Act." Mercatus Working Paper, Mercatus Center at George Mason University, Arlington, VA, August 30, 2011.

Kennedy, Peter E. *A Guide to Econometrics.* 5th ed. Cambridge, MA: MIT Press, 2003.

Keynes, John Maynard. *The Collected Writings of John Maynard Keynes*. Vol. 27, *Activities 1940–1946: Shaping the Post-War World: Employment and Commodities*. Edited by Elizabeth Johnson and Donald Moggridge. Cambridge: Cambridge University Press, 2012.

Khimm, Suzy. "Does America's 99 Percent Represent the Top 1 Percent on Earth?" *Washington Post*, October 12, 2011.

Kirzner, Israel M. *Competition and Entrepreneurship*. Chicago: University of Chicago Press, 1973.

———. *Discovery and the Capitalist Process*. Chicago: University of Chicago Press, 1985.

———. "Hayek, the Nobel, and the Revival of Austrian Economics." *Review of Austrian Economics* 28, no. 3 (September 2015): 225–36.

Kling, Arnold. *Not What They Had in Mind: A History of Policies That Produced the Financial Crisis of 2008*. Arlington, VA: Mercatus Center at George Mason University, September 2009.

———. "So You Want to Be a Masonomist." *TCS Daily*, October 17, 2007.

Knack, Stephen, and Philip Keefer. "Institutions and Economic Performance: Cross-Country Tests Using Alternative Institutional Measures." *Economics & Politics* 7, no. 3 (November 1995): 207–27.

Knight, Frank H. "Immutable Law in Economics: Its Reality and Limitations." *American Economic Review* 36, no. 2 (May 1946): 93–111.

———. *Risk, Uncertainty, and Profit*. 1921. Chicago: University of Chicago Press, 1971.

Koopman, Christopher, Matthew D. Mitchell, and Adam Thierer. "The Sharing Economy and Consumer Protection Regulation: The Case for Policy Change." *Journal of Business, Entrepreneurship & the Law* 8, no. 2 (2015): 530–45.

———. "The 'Sharing' Economy: Issues Facing Platforms, Participants, and Regulators." Public Interest Comment for Federal Trade Commission Workshop, June 9, 2015. Mercatus Center at George Mason University, Arlington, VA, May 26, 2015.

Koopmans, Tjalling C. "Measurement without Theory." *Review of Economics and Statistics* 29, no. 3 (August 1947): 161–72.

Kotlikoff, Laurence. "Assessing Fiscal Sustainability." Mercatus Research, Mercatus Center at George Mason University, Arlington, VA, December 12, 2013.

Krueger, Anne O. "The Political Economy of the Rent-Seeking Society." *American Economic Review* 64, no. 3 (1974): 291–303.

Krugman, Paul. "How Did Economists Get It So Wrong?" *New York Times Magazine*, September 2, 2009.

Kydland, Finn E., and Edward C. Prescott. "Rules Rather Than Discretion: The Inconsistency of Optimal Plans." *Journal of Political Economy* 85, no. 3 (1977): 473–92.

Lafreniere, Justin. "'Economics with Attitude' Gets High Ranking." *News at Mason*, George Mason University, February 10, 2014.

Lahart, Justin. "Economist Scraps Hepatitis Theory on China's 'Missing Women.'" *Wall Street Journal*, May 22, 2008.

Landes, David S. *The Wealth and Poverty of Nations: Why Some Are So Rich and Some So Poor.* New York: W. W. Norton, 1999.

Leamer, Edward E. "Let's Take the Con Out of Econometrics." *American Economic Review* 73, no. 1 (March 1983): 31–43.

Leeson, Peter T. *Anarchy Unbound: Why Self-Governance Works Better Than You Think.* New York: Cambridge University Press, 2014.

Levitt, Steven D. "Testing Theories of Discrimination: Evidence from 'Weakest Link.'" *Journal of Law and Economics* 47, no. 2 (2004): 431–52.

———. "Using Electoral Cycles in Police Hiring to Estimate the Effect of Police on Crime." *American Economic Review* 87, no. 3 (June 1997): 270–90.

Levitt, Steven D., and Stephen J. Dubner. *Freakonomics: A Rogue Economist Explores the Hidden Side of Everything.* New York: William Morrow, 2009.

Lind, Michael. "The Question Libertarians Just Can't Answer." *Salon.* June 4, 2013.

Locke, John. *Two Treatises of Government.* Edited by Mark Goldie. 1689. London: J. M. Dent, 1993.

Lockwood, Jim. "Moody's Views Scranton's $150M Pension Liability as Actually Closer to $250M." *Times-Tribune.* August 9, 2014.

López, Edward J, and Wayne A. Leighton. *Madmen, Intellectuals, and Academic Scribblers: The Economic Engine of Political Change.* Stanford, CA: Stanford University Press, 2012.

Lucas Jr., Robert E. "Econometric Policy Evaluation: A Critique." *Carnegie-Rochester Conference Series on Public Policy* 1, no. 1 (1976): 19–46.

———. "Expectations and the Neutrality of Money." *Journal of Economic Theory* 4, no. 2 (April 1972): 103–24.

MacAvoy, Paul W. "The Regulation-Induced Shortage of Natural Gas." *Journal of Law and Economics* 14, no. 1 (1971): 167–99.

Maddison, Angus. *The World Economy*. Paris, France: OECD, 2006.

Madison, James. "The Bank Bill, House of Representatives." 1791. In *The Founders' Constitution*. Volume 3, Article 1, Section 8, Clause 18, Document 9. Chicago: University of Chicago Press, 1987.

———. Federalist No. 10. In *The Federalist Papers*. Introduction and notes by Charles R. Kesler. Edited by Clinton Rossiter. New York: Signet Classics, 2003.

———. Federalist No. 45. In *The Federalist Papers*. Introduction and notes by Charles R. Kesler. Edited by Clinton Rossiter. New York: Signet Classics, 2003.

Martin, Nona P., and Virgil Henry Storr. "On Perverse Emergent Orders." *Studies in Emergent Order* 1 (2008): 73–91.

McCloskey, Deirdre N. *Bourgeois Dignity: Why Economics Can't Explain the Modern World*. Chicago: University of Chicago Press, 2010.

———. *Bourgeois Equality: How Ideas, Not Capital or Institutions, Enriched the World*. Chicago: University of Chicago Press, 2016.

———. *The Bourgeois Virtues: Ethics for an Age of Commerce*. Chicago: University of Chicago Press, 2006.

———. "How the West (and the Rest) Got Rich." *Wall Street Journal*, May 20, 2016.

McKelvey, Richard D. "Intransitivities in Multidimensional Voting Models and Some Implications for Agenda Control." *Journal of Economic Theory* 12, no. 3 (June 1976): 472–82.

McLaughlin, Patrick A., Matthew D. Mitchell, and Thomas Stratmann. "Does Regulation Enhance or Inhibit Turnover of Firms by Industry?" Mercatus Working Paper, Mercatus Center at George Mason University, Arlington, VA, forthcoming.

Menger, Carl. *Principles of Economics*. 1871. New York: New York University, 1981.

Milanovic, Branko. *The Haves and the Have-Nots: A Brief and Idiosyncratic History of Global Inequality*. New York: Basic Books, 2012.

Mitchell, Mark L., and Janina M. Jolley. *Research Design Explained*. 8th ed. Belmont, CA: Wadsworth Publishing, 2012.

Mitchell, Matthew D. "Ex-Im's Deadweight Loss." *Neighborhood Effects*. Mercatus Center at George Mason University, Arlington, VA, August 6, 2014.

———. *The Pathology of Privilege: The Economic Consequences of Government Favoritism*. Arlington, VA: Mercatus Center at George Mason University, 2014.

———. "Share and Share Alike: Regulatory Burdens Threaten to Overwhelm Sharing Services Like Uber and Airbnb." *U.S. News & World Report*, April 15, 2014.

———. "TEL It Like It Is: Do State Tax and Expenditure Limits Actually Limit Spending?" Mercatus Working Paper, Mercatus Center at George Mason University, Arlington, VA, December 6, 2010.

———. "Transportation Apps Offer Alternative to Taxis." *Richmond Times-Dispatch*, June 14, 2014.

———. "Trust Me on This." *Neighborhood Effects*. Mercatus Center at George Mason University, Arlington, VA, October 24, 2011.

———. "What Can Government Do to Create Jobs?" Testimony before the House Committee on Education and the Workforce, Mercatus Center at George Mason University, Arlington, VA, February 1, 2012.

———. "Why Are There No Libertarian Countries?" *Neighborhood Effects*. Mercatus Center at George Mason University, Arlington, VA, June 17, 2013.

Mitchell, Matthew D., and Michael Farren. "If You Like Uber, You Would've Loved the Jitney." *Los Angeles Times*, July 12, 2014.

Mitchell, Matthew D., and Nick Tuszynski. "Institutions and State Spending: An Overview." *Independent Review* 17, no. 1 (Summer 2012): 35–49.

Mokyr, Joel. *The Gifts of Athena: Historical Origins of the Knowledge Economy*. Princeton NJ: Princeton University Press, 2005.

Morgenson, Gretchen. *Reckless Endangerment: How Outsized Ambition, Greed, and Corruption Led to Economic Armageddon*. New York: Times Books, 2011.

Morrall III, John F., and James Broughel. "The Role of Regulatory Impact Analysis in Federal Rulemaking." Mercatus Research, Mercatus Center at George Mason University, Arlington, VA, April 10, 2014.

Mueller, Dennis C. *Public Choice III*. Cambridge: Cambridge University Press, 2003.

Mulligan, Casey B. "The Affordable Care Act and the New Economics of Part-Time Work." Mercatus Working Paper, Mercatus Center at George Mason University, Arlington, VA, October 2014.

———. *The Redistribution Recession: How Labor Market Distortions Contracted the Economy.* New York: Oxford University Press, 2012.

Murphy, Kevin M., Andrei Shleifer, and Robert W. Vishny. "The Allocation of Talent: Implications for Growth." *Quarterly Journal of Economics* 106, no. 2 (May 1991): 503–30.

Newcomb, Alyssa. "California State Sen. Leland Yee Indicted on Weapons Charges, Was Gun Control Advocate." *ABC News,* March 27, 2014.

Norcross, Eileen. "Pension Reform in Alabama: A Case for Economic Accounting." In *Improving Lives in Alabama: A Vision for Economic Freedom and Prosperity.* Troy, AL: Manuel H. Johnson Center for Political Economy at Troy University, 2014.

———. "A Reality Check on the Public Pension Crisis." *New York Times,* December 5, 2013.

Norcross, Eileen, and Andrew Biggs. "The Crisis in Public Sector Pension Plans: A Blueprint for Reform in New Jersey." Mercatus Working Paper, Mercatus Center at George Mason University, Arlington, VA, June 23, 2010.

North, Douglass C. "Economic Performance through Time." *American Economic Review* 84, no. 3 (June 1994). Quoted in *Mainline Economics: Six Nobel Lectures in the Tradition of Adam Smith.* Edited by Peter J. Boettke, Stefanie Haeffele-Balch, and Virgil Henry Storr. Arlington, VA: Mercatus Center at George Mason University, 2016.

———. *Institutions, Institutional Change and Economic Performance.* Cambridge: Cambridge University Press, 1990.

———. *Understanding the Process of Economic Change.* Princeton, NJ: Princeton University Press, 2005.

North, Douglass C., John Joseph Wallis, and Barry R. Weingast. *Violence and Social Orders.* Cambridge: Cambridge University Press, 2009.

North, Douglass C., and Barry R. Weingast. "Constitutions and Commitment: The Evolution of Institutions Governing Public Choice in Seventeenth-Century England." *Journal of Economic History* 49, no. 4 (December 1989): 803–32.

Nozick, Robert. *Anarchy, State, and Utopia.* New York: Basic Books, 1974.

Nye, John V. "The Pigou Problem." *Regulation* 31, no. 2 (Summer 2008).

Oates, Wallace E. *Fiscal Federalism.* New York: Harcourt Brace Jovanovich, 1972.

Olson, Mancur. *The Logic of Collective Action: Public Goods and the Theory of Groups.* second printing with new preface and appendix, rev. ed. Cambridge, MA: Harvard University Press, 1965.

———. *The Rise and Decline of Nations: Economic Growth, Stagflation, and Social Rigidities.* New Haven: Yale University Press, 1982.

Ostrom, Elinor. "A Behavioral Approach to the Rational Choice Theory of Collective Action: Presidential Address, American Political Science Association, 1997." *American Political Science Review* 92, no. 1 (March 1998): 1–22.

———. "Beyond Markets and States: Polycentric Governance of Complex Economic Systems." *American Economic Review* 100, no. 3 (June 2010). Quoted in *Mainline Economics: Six Nobel Lectures in the Tradition of Adam Smith.* Edited by Peter J. Boettke, Stefanie Haeffele-Balch, and Virgil Henry Storr. Arlington, VA: Mercatus Center at George Mason University, 2016.

———. *Governing the Commons: The Evolution of Institutions for Collective Action.* Cambridge: Cambridge University Press, 1990.

———. *Understanding Institutional Diversity.* Princeton, NJ: Princeton University Press, 2005.

Ostrom, Elinor, and Vincent Ostrom. "Rethinking Institutional Analysis: Interviews with Vincent and Elinor Ostrom." Interview by Paul Dragos Aligica, November 7, 2003. Mercatus Center at George Mason University, Arlington, VA, November 7, 2003.

Ostrom, Vincent. *The Intellectual Crisis in Public Administration.* Tuscaloosa: University of Alabama Press, 1973.

———. *The Meaning of Democracy and the Vulnerability of Democracies.* Ann Arbor: University of Michigan Press, 1997.

Ostrom, Vincent, and Michael Dean. "Polycentricity." In *Polycentricity and Local Public Economies: Readings from the Workshop in Political Theory and Policy Analysis.* Edited by Michael D. McGinnis. Ann Arbor: University of Michigan Press, 1999.

Ostrom, Vincent, Charles M. Tiebout, and Robert Warren. "The Organization of Government in Metropolitan Areas: A Theoretical Inquiry." *American Political Science Review* 55, no. 4 (December 1961): 831–42.

Palagashvili, Liya. "Strive to Help Entrepreneurs Thrive." *U.S. News & World Report,* April 15, 2015.

Peirce, Hester, and James Broughel. *Dodd-Frank: What It Does and Why It's Flawed.* Arlington, VA: Mercatus Center at George Mason University, 2013.

Pejovich, Svetozar. "Understanding the Transaction Costs of Transition: It's the Culture, Stupid." *Review of Austrian Economics* 16, no. 4 (2003): 347–61.

Peltzman, Sam. "The Effects of Automobile Safety Regulation." *Journal of Political Economy* 83, no. 4 (1975): 677–725.

Pigou, A. C. *The Economics of Welfare.* London: Macmillan, 1920.

Polanyi, Michael. *The Logic of Liberty.* 1951. Indianapolis: Liberty Fund, 1998.

Posner, Richard A. "Theories of Economic Regulation." *Bell Journal of Economics and Management Science* 5, no. 2 (October 1974): 335–58.

Powell, Benjamin. *Out of Poverty: Sweatshops in the Global Economy.* New York: Cambridge University Press, 2014.

Puviani, Amilcare. *Teoria della Illusione Finanziaria.* Milan: ISEDI, Istituto Editoriale Internazionale, 1903.

Rauch, Jonathan. *Government's End: Why Washington Stopped Working.* New York: PublicAffairs, 1999.

Reed, Lawrence W. "Mises and the Soviet Free Market." In *The Free Market Reader.* Edited by Llewellyn H. Rockwell Jr. Auburn, AL: Ludwig von Mises Institute, 1988.

Reifler, Jason, and Jeffrey Lazarus. "Partisanship and Policy Priorities in the Distribution of Economic Stimulus Funds." SSRN Scholarly Paper, September 1, 2010.

Ricardo, David. *On the Principles of Political Economy and Taxation.* London: John Murray, 1817.

Ridley, Matt. *The Rational Optimist: How Prosperity Evolves.* Reprint ed. New York: Harper Perennial, 2011.

Riker, William H. *Federalism: Origin, Operation, Significance.* New York: Little, Brown, 1964.

Roberts, Russ. "Gambling with Other People's Money." *Cafe Hayek.* April 28, 2010.

———. "James Heckman on Facts, Evidence, and the State of Econometrics." *EconTalk*, Library of Economics and Liberty. January 25, 2016.

Rodrik, Dani. "Institutions, Integration, and Geography: In Search of the Deep Determinants of Economic Growth." Working Paper, Weatherhead Center for International Affairs, Harvard University, February 2002.

Rodrik, Dani, Arvind Subramanian, and Francesco Trebbi. "Institutions Rule: The Primacy of Institutions over Geography and

Integration in Economic Development." *Journal of Economic Growth* 9, no. 2 (June 2004): 131–65.

Ross, Michael L. *The Oil Curse: How Petroleum Wealth Shapes the Development of Nations.* Princeton, NJ: Princeton University Press, 2013.

———. "The Political Economy of the Resource Curse." *World Politics* 51, no. 2 (January 1999): 297–322.

Ruger, William, and Jason Sorens. "Freedom in the 50 States: An Index of Personal and Economic Freedom, 2013 Edition." Mercatus Center at George Mason University, Arlington, VA, 2013.

Sachs, Jeffrey D. "Institutions Don't Rule: Direct Effects of Geography on Per Capita Income." NBER Working Paper No. 9490, National Bureau of Economic Research, February 2003.

Sachs, Jeffrey D., and Andrew M. Warner. "Economic Reform and the Process of Global Integration." *Brookings Papers on Economic Activity* 26, no. 1, 25th anniversary issue (1995): 1–118.

———. "Natural Resource Abundance and Economic Growth." NBER Working Paper No. 5398, National Bureau of Economic Research, December 1995.

Say, Jean-Baptiste. *A Treatise on Political Economy.* 1803. Philadelphia: Lippincott, Grambo & Co., 1855.

Scheiber, Noam. "Freaks and Geeks; How Freakonomics Is Ruining the Dismal Science." *New Republic*, April 2, 2007.

Schelling, Thomas C. "Models of Segregation." *American Economic Review* 59, no. 2 (May 1969): 488–93.

Schmidtz, David. *The Elements of Justice.* Cambridge: Cambridge University Press, 2006.

Schumpeter, Joseph A. *Capitalism, Socialism and Democracy.* New York: Harper & Brothers, 1942.

———. *The Theory of Economic Development: An Inquiry into Profits, Capital, Credit, Interest, and the Business Cycle.* Edited by John E. Elliott. New Brunswick, NJ: Transaction Publishers, 1934.

Seib, Gerald F. "In Crisis, Opportunity for Obama." *Wall Street Journal*, November 21, 2008.

Selgin, George, and Lawrence H. White. "A Fiscal Theory of Government's Role in Money." *Economic Inquiry* 37, no. 1 (January 1999): 154–65.

Shepsle, Kenneth A., and Barry R. Weingast. "Structure-Induced Equilibrium and Legislative Choice." *Public Choice* 37, no. 3 (January 1981): 503–19.

Simmons, Randy T. *Beyond Politics: The Roots of Government Failure.* Oakland, CA: Independent Institute, 2011.

Smiley, Gene. *The American Economy in the Twentieth Century.* Cincinnati, OH: South-Western Publishing, 1993.

Smith, Adam. *An Inquiry into the Nature and Causes of the Wealth of Nations.* 1776. Indianapolis: Liberty Fund, 1981.

———. *The Theory of Moral Sentiments.* 1759. Indianapolis: Liberty Fund, 1982.

Smith, Adam, and Bruce Yandle. *Bootleggers and Baptists: How Economic Forces and Moral Persuasion Interact to Shape Regulatory Politics.* Washington: Cato Institute, 2014.

Smith, Daniel J., and Peter J. Boettke. "An Episodic History of Modern Fed Independence." *Independent Review* 20, no. 1 (Summer 2015): 99–120.

Smith, Vernon L. *Bargaining and Market Behavior.* Cambridge: Cambridge University Press, 2000.

———. "Constructivist and Ecological Rationality in Economics." *American Economic Review* 93, no. 3 (June 2003). Quoted in *Mainline Economics: Six Nobel Lectures in the Tradition of Adam Smith.* Edited by Peter J. Boettke, Stefanie Haeffele-Balch, and Virgil Henry Storr. Arlington, VA: Mercatus Center at George Mason University, 2016.

———. "An Experimental Study of Competitive Market Behavior." *Journal of Political Economy* 70, no. 2 (April 1962): 111–37.

Smith, Vernon L., Gerry L. Suchanek, and Arlington W. Williams. "Bubbles, Crashes, and Endogenous Expectations in Experimental Spot Asset Markets." *Econometrica* 56, no. 5 (1988): 1119–51.

Sobel, Russel S., and George R. Crowley. "Do Intergovernmental Grants Create Ratchets in State and Local Taxes? Testing the Friedman-Sanford Hypothesis." Mercatus Working Paper No. 10-51, Mercatus Center at George Mason University, Arlington, VA, August 2010.

Solow, Robert M. "A Contribution to the Theory of Economic Growth." *Quarterly Journal of Economics* 70, no. 1 (February 1956): 65–94.

Steckbeck, Mark, and Peter J. Boettke. "Turning Lemons into Lemonade: Entrepreneurial Solutions in Adverse Selection Problems in E-Commerce." In *Markets, Information, and*

Communication: Austrian Perspectives on the Internet Economy. Edited by Jack Birner and Pierre Garrouste. New York: Routledge, 2004.

Stevenson, Betsey, and Justin Wolfers. "Economic Growth and Subjective Well-Being: Reassessing the Easterlin Paradox." *Brookings Papers on Economic Activity* 39, no. 1 (Spring 2008): 1–102.

Stigler, George J. "The Theory of Economic Regulation." *Bell Journal of Economics and Management Science* 2, no. 1 (Spring 1971): 3–21.

———. *The Theory of Price*. 3rd ed. New York: Macmillan, 1966.

Stock, James H., and Francesco Trebbi. "Retrospectives: Who Invented Instrumental Variable Regression?" *Journal of Economic Perspectives* 17, no. 3 (Summer 2003): 177–94.

Storr, Virgil Henry. "The Facts of the Social Sciences Are What People Believe and Think." In *Handbook on Contemporary Austrian Economics*, edited by Peter J. Boettke, 30–42. Cheltenham, UK: Edward Elgar, 2010.

———. "The Market as a Social Space: On the Meaningful Extraeconomic Conversations That Can Occur in Markets." *Review of Austrian Economics* 21, no. 2–3 (January 7, 2008): 135–50.

———. *Understanding the Culture of Markets*. New York: Routledge, 2013.

Storr, Virgil Henry, Stefanie Haeffele-Balch, and Laura E. Grube. *Community Revival in the Wake of Disaster: Lessons in Local Entrepreneurship*. New York: Palgrave Macmillan, 2015.

Stulp, Gert, Abraham Buunk, Simon Verhulst, and Thomas Pollet. "Tall Claims? Sense and Nonsense about the Importance of Height of US Presidents." *Leadership Quarterly* 24, no. 1 (February 2013).

Summers, Lawrence. "The State of the U.S. Economy." Brookings Institution Forum, Washington, DC, December 18, 2007.

Sumner, Scott. "The Case for Nominal GDP Targeting." Mercatus Research, Mercatus Center at George Mason University, Arlington, VA, October 23, 2012.

Taylor, Jason E., and Andrea Castillo. "'Timely, Targeted, and Temporary?' An Analysis of Government Expansions over the Past Century." Mercatus Research, Mercatus Center at George Mason University, Arlington, VA, January 2015.

Taylor, John. "Discretion versus Policy Rules in Practice." *Carnegie-Rochester Conference Series on Public Policy* 39, no. 1 (1993): 195–214.

———. "An Empirical Analysis of the Revival of Fiscal Activism in the 2000s." *Journal of Economic Literature* 49, no. 3 (2011): 686–702.

Thierer, Adam. *Permissionless Innovation: The Continuing Case for Comprehensive Technological Freedom.* Arlington, VA: Mercatus Center at George Mason University, 2014.

Thierer, Adam, Anne Hobson, Christopher Koopman, and Chris Kuiper. "How the Internet, the Sharing Economy and Reputational Feedback Mechanisms Solve the 'Lemons Problem.'" Mercatus Working Paper, Mercatus Center at George Mason University, Arlington, VA, May 2015.

Tiebout, Charles M. "A Pure Theory of Local Expenditures." *Journal of Political Economy* 64, no. 5 (October 1956): 416–24.

Todorov, Alexander, Anesu N. Mandisodza, Amir Goren, and Crystal C. Hall. "Inferences of Competence from Faces Predict Election Outcomes." *Science* 308, no. 5728 (June 10, 2005): 1623–26.

Tullock, Gordon. "Problems of Majority Voting." *Journal of Political Economy* 67, no. 6 (December 1959): 571–79.

———. *The Vote Motive.* Edited by Peter Kurrild-Klitgaard. London: Institute of Economic Affairs, 2006.

———. "The Welfare Costs of Tariffs, Monopolies, and Theft." *Economic Inquiry* 5, no. 3 (June 1967): 224–32.

United Nations Population Fund. "International Migration 2013." Accessed July 28, 2015.

Veenhoven, Ruut. "Is Happiness Relative?" *Social Indicators Research* 24, no. 1 (February 1991): 1–34.

Von Mises, Ludwig. *Economic Calculation in the Socialist Commonwealth.* 1920. Auburn, AL: Ludwig von Mises Institute, 1990.

———. *Human Action: A Treatise on Economics.* 1949. Indianapolis: Liberty Fund, 2010.

Wagner, Richard E. "Boom and Bust: The Political Economy of Economic Disorder." In *The Theory of Public Choice, II*, edited by James M. Buchanan and Robert D. Tollison, 238–72. Ann Arbor: University of Michigan Press, 1984.

———. *Deficits, Debt, and Democracy: Wrestling with Tragedy on the Fiscal Commons.* Cheltenham, UK: Edward Elgar, 2012.

Wagner, Richard E., and Akira Yokoyama. "Polycentrism, Federalism, and Liberty: A Comparative Systems Perspective." GMU Working Paper in Economics No. 14-10, May 10, 2014.

Weingast, Barry R. "The Economic Role of Political Institutions: Market-Preserving Federalism and Economic Growth." *Journal* of *Law, Economics, and Organization* 11, no. 1 (February 1995): 1–31.

Weinstein, Arnold A. "Transitivity of Preference: A Comparison among Age Groups." *Journal of Political Economy* 76, no. 2 (March 1968): 307–11.

Wexler, Alexandra. "Bulk of U.S. Sugar Loans Went to Three Companies." *Wall Street Journal*, June 26, 2013.

White, Lawrence H. "The Federal Reserve and the Rule of Law." Testimony before the Subcommittee on Monetary Policy and Trade, House Committee on Financial Services, Mercatus Center at George Mason University, September 11, 2013.

———. "Hayek's Monetary Theory and Policy: A Critical Reconstruction." *Journal of Money, Credit and Banking* 31, no. 1 (1999): 109–20.

White, Lawrence J. "An Assessment of the Credit Rating Agencies: Background, Analysis, and Policy." Mercatus Working Paper, Mercatus Center at George Mason University, Arlington, VA, September 10, 2013.

Wicksell, Knut. "A New Principle of Just Taxation." In *Classics in the Theory of Public Finance*, edited by Richard Musgrave and Alan Peacock, 72–118. London: Macmillan, 1958.

Williamson, Claudia R. "Informal Institutions Rule: Institutional Arrangements and Economic Performance." *Public Choice* 139, no. 3–4 (June 2009): 371–87.

Williamson, Oliver E. "Transaction-Cost Economics: The Governance of Contractual Relations." *Journal of Law and Economics* 22, no. 2 (October 1979): 233–61.

World Bank. "World Development Indicators." 2015.

Yandle, Bruce. "Bootleggers and Baptists: The Education of a Regulatory Economist." *AEI Journal on Government and Society* (June 1983).

Yandle, Bruce, Maya Vijayaraghavan, and Madhusudan Bhattarai. "The Environmental Kuznets Curve: A Primer." PERC Research Study, Property and Environmental Research Center, Bozeman, MT, May 2002.

Zywicki, Todd J., James C. Cooper, and Paul A. Pautler. "Theory and Practice of Competition Advocacy at the FTC." *Antitrust Law Journal* 72, no. 3 (2005): 1091–112.

ABOUT THE AUTHORS

Matthew D. Mitchell is a senior research fellow at the Mercatus Center at George Mason University, where he is the director of the Project for the Study of American Capitalism. He is also an adjunct professor of economics at Mason. In his writing and research, he specializes in public choice economics and the economics of government favoritism toward particular businesses, industries, and occupations.

Mitchell has testified before the US Congress and has advised several state and local government policymakers on both fiscal and regulatory policy. His research has been featured in numerous national media outlets, including the *New York Times*, the *Wall Street Journal*, the *Washington Post*, *U.S. News & World Report*, National Public Radio, and C-SPAN.

Mitchell received his PhD and MA in economics from George Mason University and his BA in political science and BS in economics from Arizona State University.

Peter J. Boettke is the vice president and director of the F. A. Hayek Program for Advanced Study in Philosophy, Politics, and Economics at the Mercatus Center as well as the BB&T Professor for the Study of Capitalism and University Professor of Economics and Philosophy at George Mason University. He specializes in Austrian economics, economic history, institutional analysis, public choice, and social change.

Boettke has authored and coauthored 11 books, including his most recent, *Living Economics*, and is editor of the *Review of Austrian Economics*, series editor of the New Thinking in Political Economy book series, and coeditor of the Cambridge Studies in Economics, Choice, and Society.

Boettke is a former Fulbright Fellow at the University of Economics in Prague, a National Fellow at Stanford University, and a Hayek Visiting Fellow at the London School of Economics. He has held visiting academic positions at the Russian Academy of Sciences in Moscow and the Stockholm School of Economics, among other institutions. Before joining the faculty at George Mason University, Boettke taught economics at New York University.

Boettke's work has earned him numerous awards, including a doctorate honoris causa in social sciences from Universidad Francisco Marroquín in Guatemala and an honorary doctorate from Alexandru Ioan Cuza University in Romania.

Boettke received his PhD in economics from George Mason University.

ACKNOWLEDGMENTS

Our manuscript benefited from a great many helpful suggestions and edits from Paul Dragos Aligica, James Broughel, Garrett Brown, Rosolino Candela, Carrie Conko, Tyler Cowen, Veronique de Rugy, Jerry Ellig, Stefanie Haeffele-Balch, Angela Kuck, Eileen Norcross, McKenzie Robey, Solomon Stein, Virgil Storr, Adam Thierer, TJ Whittle, Richard Williams, and Kaitlyn Woltz. We owe a special debt to Richard Williams for conceiving this project and for convincing us that it was worthwhile. We are responsible for any errors or omissions that remain.

INDEX

capital
  allocation, 39–40
  defined, 39
  intangible capital as
    percentage of, 107n64
Caplan, Bryan, 72
Castillo, Andrea, 84
catallactics, 32–33, 55
central banks, 41, 113n26,
  113n30
Chamlee-Wright, Emily, 44
Chetty, Raj, 15
Chicago price theory, 91–92
Clark, Gregory, 6
Coase, Ronald
  Chicago price theory, 91
  FCC paper, 24–25
  George Mason University,
    influence on, 91
  Hayek's challenge, response
    to, 88
  mainline economics, 3, 21
  Nobel Prize lecture, 50
  on transaction costs, 50, 51,
    52–53
Code of Federal Regulations, 80
collective action problem, 80
common-pool resources, 26, 62
competition
  as process of entrepreneurial
    discovery, 36–38, 95
  unleashing of, 43–44
Conover, Christopher, 65
constitutional political
    economy, 59–60
costs and benefits. *See* benefits
    and costs
Cowen, Tyler, 93
Coyne, Christopher, 55, 71
crime, 9

crises, producing change, 45
Crowley, George, 84
culture
  as capital, 56
  institutions and, 49–68
  market exchange and, 55–57
  shaping economic prosperity,
    16–17
Culture of Markets (Storr), 16–17

de Rugy, Veronique, 81–82,
    83, 84
deregulation, unleashing
    dynamic competition, 43
Diamond, Jared, 5–6
difference-in-differences
    analysis, 10–11
disaster recovery, 44
division of labor, 20
Donohue, John, 11
Doucouliagos, Chris, 58
dynamism
  entrepreneurship, 43–44
  in market process, 3, 20, 21
  regulatory impact analysis, 81

Easterlin, Richard, 101n10
Easterlin paradox, 101n10
economic freedom, 58, 94
economic growth
  benefits of, 4
  defined, 4
  economic freedom and, 58
  sources of, 14
  unproductive
    entrepreneurship and,
    118n30
economic prosperity, 1–17
  benefits of, 4–5, 101n10
  culture's impact on, 16–17

Made in the USA
Middletown, DE
31 July 2023